The Reed Trio:
An Annotated Bibliography
of Original
Published Works

The Reed Trio: An Annotated Bibliography of Original Published Works

by James E. Gillespie, Jr.

Detroit Studies in
Music Bibliography-20

Information Coordinators, Inc.
Detroit, 1971

INFORMATION COORDINATORS, INC.
1435-37 Randolph Street
Detroit, Michigan 48226

DETROIT STUDIES IN MUSIC BIBLIOGRAPHY

.... Bruno Nettl, General Editor

DETROIT STUDIES IN MUSIC BIBLIOGRAPHY

.... Bruno Nettl, General Editor

AN ANNOTATED BIBLIOGRAPHY OF WOODWIND INSTRUC-
TION BOOKS, 1600-1830, by Thomas E. Warner
1967 138p $3.00   Number 11

WORKS FOR SOLO VOICE OF JOHANN ADOLPH HASSE
(1699-1783), by Sven Hostrup Hansell 1968 110p
$3.00   Number 12

A SELECTED DISCOGRAPHY OF SOLO SONG, by Dorothy
Stahl 1970 95p $2.50
SUPPLEMENT, 1968-1969 1970 95p $2.50   Number 13

MUSIC PUBLISHING IN CHICAGO BEFORE 1871: THE FIRM
OF ROOT & CADY, 1858-1871, by Dena J. Epstein
1969 243p $6.00   Number 14

AN INTRODUCTION TO CERTAIN MEXICAN MUSICAL
ARCHIVES, by Lincoln Spiess and Thomas Stanford
1969 85+99p $3.50   Number 15

A CHECKLIST OF AMERICAN MUSIC PERIODICALS, 1850-
1900, by William J. Weichlein 1970 103p $3.00   Number 16

A CHECKLIST OF TWENTIETH-CENTURY CHORAL MUSIC
FOR MALE VOICES, by Kenneth Roberts 1970 32p
$2.00   Number 17

PUBLISHED MUSIC FOR THE VIOLA DA GAMBA AND
OTHER VIOLS, by Robin de Smet 1971 105p $3.00   Number 18

THE WORKS OF CHRISTOPH NICHELMANN: A THEMATIC
INDEX, by Douglas A. Lee 1971 100p $3.50   Number 19

CONTENTS

ACKNOWLEDGEMENTS

THE PRESENT study could not have been completed without the assistance and cooperation of many persons. The writer wishes to thank the following for their help in playing and taping the works included in this project: Judyth Stysh, graduate student in oboe, Indiana University; Jack Sharp, graduate student in bassoon, Indiana University; Pat Wilson, undergraduate woodwinds major, University of Redlands (California); and John Winter, undergraduate oboe major, University of Redlands (California). Special appreciation is expressed to Herbert Oberlag, Assistant Professor of Music at Southern Illinois University, for the loan of many scores from his personal library. Also, without the financial assistance in the form of a grant-in-aid from Indiana University, the project could not have been finished. Two European publishers were particularly cooperative in supplying examination scores, Donemus of Holland and the Belgian Center for Music Documentation (CeBeDeM). Dr. Dominique-René deLerma, Music Librarian of the Indiana University School of Music, was very helpful in securing scores from foreign sources, and virtually every member of the woodwind faculty of the Indiana University School of Music contributed ideas regarding annotation topics. The writer is particularly indebted to Dr. Eugene Rousseau, Associate Professor of Music at Indiana University, not only for the initial idea of an annotated bibliography, but also for his guidance of this study through all of its phases.

J. E. G.

INTRODUCTION

THERE HAS been a significant increase in the composition and performance of music for wind instruments in the twentieth century with virtually every instrument and instrumental combination provided with an expanded and improved repertory.

In the area of woodwind instruments, one combination, in particular, has benefited from this development: the woodwind quintet, comprised of flute, oboe, clarinet, bassoon, and French horn. Although works for this medium date back to the late eighteenth century, compositions written for it since 1900 number in the hundreds, and some of them, such as Paul Hindemith's Kleine Kammermusik, Op. 24, No. 2 (copyright 1922), are among the best known examples of wind chamber music.

The repertory of another woodwind ensemble from within the quintet has also developed considerably, but it has been almost forgotten by many performers. The reed trio, made up of oboe, clarinet, and bassoon, has been greatly overshadowed by the woodwind quintet, but, in terms of the number of original works, it ranks second only to the quintet in woodwind chamber music.

OBJECTIVE OF THE STUDY

The present listing of works for the reed trio has been undertaken to assist musicians, particularly woodwind players, high school band directors, and college woodwind ensemble coaches, in surveying the literature for the medium. Only compositions for the specific medium of oboe, clarinet, and bassoon are included, although in some cases scores which indicate optional instrumentation, such as oboe (flute), clarinet, and bassoon are listed. In instances where the score designates either the oboe, clarinet, or bassoon as an optional instrument, the works are not originally for the medium, and thus are not included in the present study.

Among the most common names given to the woodwind ensemble of oboe, clarinet, and bassoon are reed trio, trio d'anches, and woodwind trio. For clarity as well as consistency, the term "reed trio" is used in this paper in preference to the less familiar trio d'anches (French), and the ambiguous, woodwind trio.

Another limitation set for this study is the inclusion of available published works only, which the writer defines as compositions whose scores and/or individual parts have been reproduced and are accessible for purchase by the public. Thus, works that are out of print, and works available only on a rental basis, are not considered. Every attempt has been made to make the bibliography as complete as possible including works published through 1968.

Although this study indicates that a substantial repertory, worthy of both study and performance, exists for the reed trio, two limitations in its literature should be noted. Since the available works encompass only the years 1897 to 1968, there is a lack of historical and stylistic range in the repertory; also, there is a significant shortage of works, both in number and quality, at the lower grade levels. Nevertheless, it is hoped that this study will create more interest in the reed trio and in other woodwind ensembles that have not become as well known as the woodwind quintet.

HISTORICAL OVERVIEW

The earliest published work for the reed trio was written by the French clarinetist Jean-Xavier Lefèvre (1763-1829), who served as Professor of Clarinet at the Paris Conservatory from 1795 to 1825. It is titled Concertante and was published by the Paris firm of Janet (date unknown).[1] The company is no longer in existence and the piece is not available.

The earliest composition for the medium that is still in print is the Trio by Ange Flégier (1846-1927) written in 1897 and published in Paris by Gallet. No date of copyright or publication is indicated on the score. This work, and its recent revision, will be discussed in detail in its entry in the bibliography.

Introductie en fuga, written by the Dutch composer John Johannes, is the most recent, published work for the reed trio in this study. It was written in 1968 and published by Donemus (copyright date also in 1968), and is included in the annotations below.

The available works for this medium, then, encompass the years 1897 to 1968, but it was not until the 1930's that the repertory began to develop substantially with the founding of the Editions de L'Oiseau-Lyre by the late Louise B. M. Dyer-Hanson. Her widower, J. B. Hanson, has provided the writer with an account of her interest in the reed trio:

> She was Australian and a woman of superb talents. Liking the sonority of the Reed Trio, that is, quite simply, the noise it made, she decided to put out phonograph records. But there was little music for this combination. So she asked the composers you mention (they were personal acquaintances of course) to write trios. When I say the composers were acquaintances, you must understand that Louise Dyer, though Australian, lived in Paris and was well known in the world of music. Most of the trios were written, published and recorded in the period 1934-1939. Since then, of course, the reed combination has been taken up all over the world.[2]

*　　*　　*

1. Fétis, F. J., Biographie universelle des musiciens et bibliographie générale de la musique, vol. 5, p. 253.
2. Personal letter written by J. B. Hanson to the writer on February 19, 1969.

The composers involved in these commissions were Georges Auric (1899–   ), Henri Barraud (1900–   ), Joseph Canteloube (1879-1957), Jacques Ibert (1890-1962), Boyan Ikonomow (1900–   ), Daniel Lesur (1908–   ), Darius Milhaud (1892–   ), and Henri Sauget (1901–   ).

Another important factor in the development of the reed trio's repertory was the formation of the Trio d'Anches de Paris by Fernand Oubradous (1903–   ) in the 1930's. The personnel included Myrtil Morel, oboe, Pierre Lefèbvre, clarinet, and Oubradous, bassoon, and this ensemble is the earliest reed trio to which works were dedicated. Apparently it has since disbanded because no works have been dedicated to them since the late 1930's. Oubradous is now active as a conductor, composer, and arranger. [3] The scores of eleven works bear a dedication to the Trio d'Anches de Paris.

Barraud, Henri	Trio
Bozza, Eugène	Fughette, sicilienne, rigaudon
Foret, Félicien	Suite
Franck, Maurice	Trio
Goué, Emile	Trois pièces en trio: bagatelle, mélopée, scherzo
Ibert, Jacques	Cinq pièces en trio
Milhaud, Darius	Pastorale
Orban, Marcel	Prelude, pastorale, divertissement
Tomasi, Henri	Concert Champêtre
Rivier, Jean	Petite suite
Roussel, Albert	Andante

All of these works will be discussed in more detail in the annotations below. All of them remain in print, except for the Andante by Roussel written in 1937 and published by Leduc (no date). It was published as the only complete movement from the composer's Trio which was left unfinished at the composer's death. [4]

Another important professional reed trio was the René Daraux Trio d'Anches which, according to the dates of most of the works written for them, was apparently most active during the 1940's. It was made up of Daraux, oboe, Fernand Gossens, clarinet, and Ange Maugendre, bassoon. The works dedicated to them include:

Bull, Hagerup	Trois bucoliques
Canteloube, Joseph	Rustiques
Constant, Marius	Trio
d'Harcourt, M. Beclard	Rapsodie Péruvienne
Poot, Marcel	Ballade

*   *   *

3. Oubradou's Sonatine for reed trio published by Selmer (date unknown) is out of print.
4. Cobbett, W. W., Cobbett's Cyclopedic Survey of Chamber Music, vol. 3, p. 29.

11

Sauget, Henri	<u>T r i o</u>
Spisak, Michal	<u>S o n a t i n a</u>
Szalowski, Anton	<u>D i v e r t i m e n t o</u>
Thiriet, Maurice	<u>L a i s e t v i r e l a i s</u>

Other ensembles for which works have been written include: the <u>G e n t s e</u> <u>H o u t b l a z e r s - t r i o</u> of Belgium; <u>A n d r é</u> <u>D u p o n t</u> <u>T r i o d ' A n c h e s</u> (Paul Taillefer, oboe, André Gabry, clarinet, and Dupont, bassoon); <u>R o t t e r d a m</u> <u>W i n d e n s e m b l e</u> (Cees van den Bergh, oboe, Gerrit Kryt, clarinet, Henk de Wit, bassoon); <u>T o l e d o</u> <u>W o o d w i n d</u> <u>T r i o</u>; <u>T r i o</u> <u>S t o t ỹ n</u>, <u>O p s t a l</u>, <u>S t o t ỹ n</u> of Holland; <u>B r u s s e l s</u> <u>W i n d</u> <u>T r i o</u>; <u>T r i o d ' A n c h e s</u> <u>d e</u> <u>B e l g i q u e</u>; and the <u>B e r k s h i r e</u> <u>W o o d w i n d</u> <u>E n s e m b l e</u>.

Since the initial development of the reed trio's repertory was in France, it is not surprising that a large number of compositions written for the medium has come from French composers. The composers who have contributed the most works to the repertory have come from France, Belgium, Holland, and the United States. The most important publishers of works for the reed trio are L'Oiseau-Lyre, Alphonse Leduc of Paris, Donemus of Holland, Maurer of Belgium, and the Belgian Center for Music Documentation, which will be referred to in this study by its abbreviation Ce BeDeM.

ORGANIZATION OF THE BIBLIOGRAPHY

The annotated list of compositions for reed trio is organized as follows: (1) composer's name, (2) composer's dates and nationality, (3) title of composition, (4) score availability, (5) timing, (6) location and name of publisher, (7) date of composition or copyright, (8) level of difficulty, (9) movement titles and/or tempo indications, (10) style, and (11) performance considerations.

The composer's name, arranged alphabetically by the last name, is listed as it appears on the title page of the score, except in cases where only the first initial of the composer's given name is indicated on the score; then, both the last name and the given name are listed for reasons of consistency. The surname appears first, followed by the given name. The year of the composer's birth, and death when applicable, is included in parentheses immediately following the name of the composer. Although every attempt has been made to include the dates of every composer represented in this study, in a few cases this information was not available. The name of the composer's native country is given after his dates; in instances where the composer is associated stylistically with a country other than, or in addition to, that in which he was born, the names of both countries appear (native country first).

The complete title of each composition is listed as it appears on the title page of the score; an asterisk (*) immediately preceding the first word of the title indicates that a full score is published. The title is followed by a timing in minutes and seconds of the complete work. In cases where this information does not appear on the score, it has been determined by the writer in playing the work.

The location and name of the publisher are given as they appear on the title page of the score. If two editions of the same work are available, the publisher with the earlier edition is indicated first. This is followed by the date of composition, or in instances where this information has not been determined, the date of copyright is indicated by a "c" before the date.

Grading of the difficulty is indicated by a Roman numeral, according to the following scale:

I-II   Easy, elementary school
III-IV   Intermediate, junior and senior high school
V-VI   Advanced, college and professional

It should be noted that works that require clarinet in A in the III, IV, or III-IV grade levels may not always be practical for high school use. High school clarinet players do not always own, or have access to, a clarinet in A.

The titles of the movements and/or tempo designations (Allegro, Andante, etc.) are listed in the sequence in which they occur in the work.

The brief description of the musical style of each work deals primarily with melody, harmony, rhythm, and texture. In some cases annotations are taken from periodical reviews, composer's comments in the score, or descriptions provided by composers specifically for this bibliography. If the score bears a dedication, this information is also provided.

Among the items considered in summarizing the principal performance considerations of each work are:

1. technical facility
2. instrumental pitch range
3. rhythmic complexity
4. ensemble precision
5. balance of interest among the parts
6. balance of difficulty among the parts
7. tempi
8. articulation
9. endurance
10. legibility of the score
11. printing errors
12. type of clarinet required (B-flat or A)

In order to clarify references to specific pitches for the instruments, the octave segmentation below will be used:

Unless otherwise noted, the instrumentation for each work is oboe, clarinet in B-flat, and bassoon.

ANNOTATED BIBLIOGRAPHY OF WORKS

ARMA, PAUL (1904-   ): Czechoslovakia; France
  Trois mouvements (10:00). Paris: Editions Musicales Transatlantiques (c1960)   (Grade V-VI)
    I. Polyphone
    II. Homophone
    III. Intermodal
The influence of Arma's teacher, Béla Bartók, is evident throughout,
particularly with regard to the rhythmic aspect of the work. Syncopated
rhythmic figures, irregular accents, and cross rhythms[5] are employed,
especially in the third movement. The titles of the first two movements
suggest the prevailing texture for each, while the wide variety of modal
melodies used in the last movement is indicated by its title.

The most difficult technical problems are present in the third
movement where the modal-based thematic material, often written in the
instruments' most extreme registers, is not easy to execute. Arma also
makes considerable use of the extreme upper register of the oboe calling
for g^3 on several occasions in the third movement. There are solo
passages for all three instruments throughout the work.

ARRIEU, CLAUDE (1903-   ): France
  *Trio en ut (10:10). Paris: Amphion (1948)   (Grade V-VI)
    I. Allegro
    II. Pastorale et scherzo
    III. Final
One of four works for the medium by a female composer, this piece is
stylistically conservative, highly spirited, and very light in character. The
title indicates a tonal idiom, but chromatic chords, unexpected accidentals,
and abrupt modulations are common. The oboe dominates most of the
melodic material, and its expressive capability, versatility, and virtuoso
potential are fully exploited.

The virtuosity alluded to applies equally to the instruments, not just
the oboe. The technical demands in the Scherzo and the Final are very
advanced, particularly at the composer's recommended metronome markings.
The accompanimental passages are angular and wide-ranging in the bassoon.

AURIC, GEORGES (1899-   ): France
  Trio (12:00). Paris: L'Oiseau-Lyre (c1948)   (Grade VI)
    I. Décidé
    II. Romance
    III. Final

                    *   *   *

5. The term "cross rhythm" will be used in this study in reference to
rhythmic groupings that tend to negate the indicated meter signature
and establish the feeling of another meter. For instance, in the
following example 9/8 is heard as the prevailing meter rather than 2/4:

𝄴 ♫♫ ♪♫♫♪♫♫ etc.

17

AURIC, GEORGES (1899-   ): France (Continued)

Commissioned by Louise B. M. Dyer-Hanson and dedicated to Henri Sauget, this is one of the best known and most often performed works for the medium. Its light, witty character, lively tempi and rhythms, attractive melodies, and overall brilliance are the most obvious features of its style.

This work requires players with expert technique, fast articulation, and command of the full range of their respective instruments. The clarinet and oboe are particularly prominent in the first and last movements, while both double-reed instruments are featured in the Romance. There are several awkward technical passages for the clarinet in the outer movements, and the use of the extreme upper and lower registers is a serious problem for the oboist. Clarinet in A is required throughout.

BADINGS, HENK (1907-   ): Holland

*Trio (16:00). Amsterdam: Donemus (1943)   (Grade V)
  I.   Allegro
  II. Scherzo
  III. Tema con variazioni
  IV. Rondo (Allegro)

For the most part, Badings "favors a more sombre and chromatically more intense harmony, and has sometimes used a system based on a scale of alternating major and minor seconds. "[6] The prevailing texture throughout the work is homophonic, and many passages are scored in a concerted manner. The three variations of the third movement are of the melodic type. All of the fast movements are light in character and highly rhythmical.

The unusual scale materials create awkward finger combinations. The oboist must have good control of the altissimo register, particularly in the Scherzo. The rhythms are straightforward, and ensemble precision is not particularly problematic.

BAEYENS, AUGUST LOUIS (1895-1966): Belgium

*Concertino (13:00). Antwerp: Metropolis (1951)   (Grade V-VI)
  I.   Allegro
  II. Andante
  III. Cadenza; Alla marcia

From a compositional standpoint, Baeyens manages to combine elements of tonality, polytonality, and atonality. The melodic writing is equally diverse with the interval of the fourth being very prominent. An imitative texture is maintained throughout most of the first two movements, while the march section of the last movement is preceded by short cadenzas in oboe, bassoon, and clarinet respectively.

The independent character of each of the parts in this work complicates ensemble precision. Much of the bassoon part is in the tenor range. The cadenzas in the last movement require advanced technical facility in each part.

*   *   *

6. Cobbett, W. W., Cobbett's Cyclopedic Survey of Chamber Music, vol. 3, p. 80.

BARRAUD, HENRI (1900-   ): France
   Trio (9:30). Paris: L'Oiseau-Lyre (c1938)   (Grade IV-V)
      I. Allegro
      II. Andante
      III. Rondo
Dedicated to the Trio d'Anches de Paris, this is another in the
series of works commissioned by Louise B. M. Dyer-Hanson. Its emphasis
is on cantabile melodic writing shared in all three instruments. The texture
is varied throughout with short solo passages interspersed with sections in a
more contrapuntal character. Rhythmic interest is sustained through the use
of a wide variety of rhythmic figures.
   Rhythmic ensemble precision is somewhat complicated by the wide variety
of rhythmic figures presented, but the technical demands made upon the players
are only moderately advanced. Clarinet in A is required throughout.

BARTSCH, CHARLES (1916-   ): Belgium
   *Suite (9:00). Brussels: Maurer (1965)   (Grade IV-V)
      I. Serioso
      II. Giocoso
      III. Pomposo
      IV. Strepitoso
Bartsch's style is similar in many ways to that of other Belgian composers
of works for the reed trio. A variety of textures is employed, with frequent
use made of contrapuntal sections. Vertical sonorities are rarely triadic,
and tonal centers are only fleetingly suggested. The titles of the movements
serve to suggest their general character.
   Although technical demands are not of virtuoso proportions, the angular
thematic material in the fast movements will require flexibility and light,
rapid articulation from all three players. Intricate ensemble precision is a
factor only in the last movement. There is a balance of interest and technical
difficulty among the parts.

BAUERNFIEND, HANS (1908-   ): Germany
   *Heitere Musik (13:15). Vienna: Doblinger (1955)   (Grade IV)
      I. Mässig bewegt
      II. Langsam, sehr ausdrucksvoll
      III. Lebhaft
The score indicates that this work is "für drei Instrumente, " and the
composer suggests one of two possible combinations for performance: violin,
viola, and cello, or oboe, clarinet in A, and bassoon. Parts for each
instrument are included. The pleasant mood suggested by the title is maintained
throughout the work, and Bauernfiend's style is conservative, rhythmically
uncomplicated, melodious, and well balanced in formal organization. The
outer movements are both cast in a three-part form, and the principal theme,
scored in octaves, is presented at the beginning of each movement. The
prevailing key of the trio is D major.

19

BAUERNFIEND, HANS (1908–   ): Germany (Continued)
Although the composer recommends wind instruments to perform this piece, the writing seems more suitable for strings, and less idiomatic for the reed instruments. That strings were conceived as the primary media is suggested by the fact that the publisher's full score lists the strings first and the winds in parentheses. Technical demands are not severe, but endurance could be a factor since all three instruments are playing most of the time. Problems in ensemble are minimal, and there is an interesting musical balance among the parts.

BAUMANN, HERBERT (1931–   ): Germany
    Divertimento (9:00). Hamburg: Sikorski (c1961)   (Grade IV-V)
        I. Sonatina (Allegro)
        II. Aria (Andante)
        III. Ostinato (Allegretto)
        IV. Variazioni (canto populare tedesco) (Allegro)
    This highly melodious work combines lively rhythms, balance among the instruments, and formal clarity. The titles of the last three movements indicate their style or formal organization. The Ostinato opens with a lengthy statement of the theme in bassoon, followed by successive entrances in clarinet and oboe. A lively folk theme serves as the basis for a set of free, continuous variations in the last movement; the theme is first stated in bassoon in E major and is elaborated through a number of changes of key and meter. A cyclic feature occurs near the end of the work with the recurrence of the theme of the Sonatina. In a somewhat humorous vein, the clarinet closes the work with a diminuendo statement of the folk theme.
    Except for a somewhat more difficult bassoon part, the instruments are equally balanced.

BENTZON, JORGEN (1897–1951): Denmark
    *Racconto No. 3, Op. 31 (12:00). Copenhagen: Skandinvisk og
    Borups (c1937)   (Grade IV-V)
    This one-movement work is in a large three-part design with the opening "A" section returning somewhat modified at the end of the piece. It shows the post-romantic influence of Carl Nielsen, Bentzon's teacher, and the harmonies are somewhat dissonant, although always tonally organized. Emphasis is placed upon the lyric, cantabile qualities of the instruments, and each one is usually very independent of the others.
    The oboe and clarinet carry most of the melodic material with a lengthy solo passage for oboe occurring before the recapitulation of the opening section. The more difficult technical passages are in the clarinet part. The occasional use of 5/4 meter and duplet rhythmic groupings in 6/8 meter present little difficulty. The subtle changes in tempo during the transitions between the major sections of the work could present problems to less experienced players. Clarinet in A is required throughout.

BERTOUILLE, GÉRARD (1898-   ): Belgium
   *Prélude et fugue (3:30). Brussels: CeBeDeM (1957)   (Grade IV-V)
      I. Prélude
     II. Fugue
Both movements of this short work are atonal and contrapuntal. The
first movement is more lyric and less abstract than the second movement,
and the long crescendo and diminuendo in the former are a challenge for the
performers to effect. The Fugue is rather free in form with successive
statements of the subject in oboe, clarinet, and bassoon.
   The Fugue is the more technically challenging of the two movements, but
the composer's suggested tempo is well within the capabilities of many
high school players. The angular, chromatic melodic lines make for difficult
reading, however. Clarinet in A is required throughout.

BODER, GERD (   )
   *Trio, Op. 1 (12:00). Leipzig: N. Simrock (c1965)   (Grade VI)
      I. Allegretto
     II. Chaconne
    III. Valse
     IV. Finale
The most striking features of this work are its atonal idiom, extremely
angular themes, and varied rhythmic content. The opening theme, stated in
octaves, shows a twelve-tone technique influence, as all twelve chromatic
pitches are present. However, the organization does not appear to be serial,
and some passages with 'ostinati' figures tend to emphasize some pitches as
temporary, harmonic focal points. All of the movements are in a loose
ternary form, and multimeters[7] are present only in the first two movements.
   The stylistic considerations mentioned above require three expert
players to bring this work off in performance. Not only is the rhythmic
ensemble difficult, but the wide-ranging, disjunct themes demand even more
attention to flexibility and control.

BONNEAU, PAUL (1918-   ): France
   Trois noëls anciens (2:30). Paris: Leduc (c1949)   (Grade III)
This short work in one movement presents a straightforward, chordal
setting of three old Christmas carols. The first of these is more modal than
the others, and the oboe is featured. Each instrument carries the melodic
line at one point or another in the remaining carols, and the notational use
of brackets to frame the primary melodies will be of help to younger players.
The score indicates that either English horn or clarinet may be used, and
parts for each are included.

                    *   *   *

7. The term "multimeter" is used in this study to describe frequent and
extended use of more than one meter signature within the line.

21

BONNEAU, PAUL (1918-   ): France (Continued)
The key signature of five sharps for the clarinet in the final carol, and
the low register scoring in oboe will offer some challenges to young students;
the work, as a whole, should help to develop good habits of ensemble playing.
Also, its melodic origins should have some seasonal appeal.

BOOREN, JO van den (1935-   ): Holland
  *Trio, Op. 2 (10:15). Amsterdam: Donemus (1960)   (Grade V-VI)
    I. Andante
    II. Lento
    III. Scherzino
    IV. Fugato
The opening movement is in ternary form and features an animated
middle section that closes with a brilliant oboe cadenza. The thematic
material of the Lento is quite fragmentary, the resulting texture being
very thin and pointillistic. Lively melodic material in the third movement is carried primarily in the oboe, with the contrasting middle section
of the movement and the slower-paced themes shared equally in all
three instruments. A high degree of chromaticism prevails throughout
the work, while the fugue subject of the last movement is typical of
the composer's melodic style with its unexpected turns in harmonic
direction.
Although the first and third movements present the greatest challenge
in technical facility, the entire piece demands careful attention to ensemble
precision due to the independent character of the parts and the frequent
contrapuntal passages.

BOURGUIGNON, FRANCIS de (1890-   ): Belgium
  *Suite en trio, Op. 80 (14:00). Brussels: CeBeDeM (1944)
                                            (Grade V)
    I. Prélude
    II. Scherzo
    III. Fugato
    IV. Finale
Typical of many of the works for reed trio by modern Belgian composers,
this trio features a variety of melodic and rhythmic materials within a
prevailing atonal framework. Each of the four movements is unique in
mood and harmony: the first is lyric and modal, featuring the oboe; the
second is atonal and thematically disjunct; the third is contrapuntal and more
tonal than the other movements; the final movement is light, tuneful, and
rhythmic.
Technical requirements are somewhat challenging in this Suite, and
the second movement is particularly awkward for clarinet. Endurance is a
factor in the third movement for all three instruments, and the syncopated
rhythmic style of the Finale requires precise ensemble.

BOUTRY, ROGER (1932-   ): France
    *Divertissement (10:15). Paris: Leduc (c1956)   (Grade VI)
        I. Jeux
        II. Dialogue
        III. Ronde
    The title of the first movement suggests its light, playful character,
while Dialogue is more atonal and dissonant. The last movement is built
largely upon a six-note rhythmic grouping that appears both in the principal
melodic material and accompanimental figures. A wide variety of scales
is employed with major-minor types prevailing. Although key signatures
are present, tonal centers are evident only at the end of the movements, the
harmonic vocabulary being quite chromatic.
    Ensemble rhythmic precision is complicated due, in large measure, to
the multimeters in each movement. Technical facility is demanding in all
the parts, but particularly for the oboe in the Ronde. Much of the bassoon
part is in tenor range, and several passages are scored in octaves between
oboe and bassoon.

BOVE, J. HENRY (1897-1963): France
    *Petit Trio (2:30). New York: Carl Fischer (c1934)   (Grade III)
    This unpretentious little piece can also be performed by flute,
clarinet, and bassoon as specified in the score. It is dedicated to the
American composer Lamar Stringfield, and it could well serve as a
training work for younger students. It is quite conservative in every
respect with a note-against-note style prevailing. Each of the instruments
shares the melodic material. The bassoon opens the work with a
short cadenza.
    Except for a few passages involving altissimo-register playing for
clarinet, there is a minimum number of technical problems encountered
in the work.

BOZZA, EUGÈNE (1905-   ): France
    *Fughette, sicilienne, rigaudon (7:15). Paris: Paul Richard
    (1933)   (Grade V-VI)
        I. Fughette (Allegro vivace)
        II. Sicilienne (Moderato)
        III. Rigaudon (Vif)
    The titles of the movements suggest their character and rhythmic style;
and, except for occasional dissonant harmonies and angular melodies, the
other aspects of the work are influenced by the baroque period. For instance,
the closing measures of the first movement contain a sustained pedal point
in bassoon, plagal cadence, and an ornamented resolution of a suspension in
the other parts. The work is dedicated to the Trio d'Anches de Paris.
    This work requires advanced technique and rapid articulation in the
Rigaudon. Much of the bassoon part is in tenor range and notated in treble
clef.

23

BOZZA, EUGÈNE (1905-   ):   France (Continued)
*Suite brève en trio, Op. 67 (10:30).   Paris: Leduc (c1947)

(Grade VI)
    I.   Allegro moderato
    II. Allegro vivo
    III. Adagio espressivo
    IV. Final

As in Bozza's more recent woodwind works, this suite features rapid chromatic scales, modal harmonies, oriental effects through the use of pentatonic scales, syncopated jazz rhythms, and an overall emphasis on brilliance.   Brackets are also employed in the notation to enclose important melodic material, although this practice seems unnecessary for the calibre of players required to play the piece.

Demanding technique, complex rhythm, rapid articulation, and complete control of a wide dynamic range are the most critical challenges to the performers of this work.

BRONS, CAREL (1931-   ): Holland
*Serenata 2 (4:15).   Amsterdam: Donemus (1964)   (Grade V-VI)

This short, one-movement work employs serial organization of the pitch element in certain sections, with the resultant melodic style being angular and wide in range.   The texture is primarily contrapuntal, but several measures are chordal.   Thematic and formal cohesion is not readily apparent.

In a work with this degree of rhythmic complexity, it is unfortunate that all of the parts are not printed in score form; this would greatly simplify problems in ensemble precision.   Except for control of wide intervals, technical problems are not extremely demanding.

BULL, EDVARD HAGERUP (1922-   ): Norway
*Trois bucoliques (10:00).   Paris: Amphion (1964)   (Grade V-VI)
    I.   Allegretto
    II. Andante con moto
    III. Final

Although the pastoral or rustic quality implied in the title is not always clearly evident in the music, a light, cheerful, and rhythmically spirited mood does prevail.   The variety of rhythmic figures is extremely wide, and all three movements are scattered with grace notes and dotted rhythmic figures.   Chromaticism is common; the thematic material is angular, and oftentimes syncopated.   The work is dedicated to the René Daraux Trio d'Anches.

The most challenging aspects of the work are its formidable technical demands, complex rhythmic style, and endurance in the double reeds in the middle movement.   Oboe and bassoon are the most frequently featured instruments, and their material is often scored in their most extreme registers.   The subtle changes in tempo indicated in the first movement would also be difficult to coordinate in ensemble.

CANTELOUBE, JOSEPH (1879-1957): France
Rustiques (15:00). Paris: L'Oiseau-Lyre (1946)   (Grade V-VI)
    I. Pastorale
    II. Rêverie
    III. Rondeau à la française
Written in the post-romantic style of his teacher, Vincent d'Indy, this work is characterized by its rich harmonies, varied moods and tempi within movements, and melodies frequently based on modes. Canteloube also uses rhythmic 'ostinati' as an accompanying device. The work is dedicated to the René Daraux Trio d'Anches.
    Although all of the instruments are featured in a solo capacity from time to time, the oboe is the most prominent. The writing, in general, is quite idiomatic and technically challenging. The second movement presents some endurance problems for oboe, and its extreme low register is utilized in many passages requiring sensitive control by the oboist. The most critical problem, though, is adjusting to the many changes in mood and tempo within each movement. In other words, this work requires players with a high degree of musical maturity.

CHEMIN-PETIT, HANS (1902-): Germany
*Trio im alten Stil (20:00). Berlin: Lienau (c1944)
                                                    (Grade V)
    I. Allegro con spirito
    II. Andante sostenuto
    III. Menuetto; Trio
    IV. Allegretto con moto (Doppelfuge mit dem Lied "Kume, kum Geselle min")
Sequential melodies, 4-3 suspensions at many cadences, and ornamentation are all in abundance in this work, and the "old style" mentioned in the title apparently is the baroque period. This aspect of the work is similar to Eugène Bozza's Fughette, sicilienne, rigaudon discussed above, although Chemin-Petit's harmonic idiom is more conservative and less dissonant than Bozza's. A contrapuntal texture prevails throughout the last movement. The work is dedicated to the publishers, Robert and Rosemarie Lienau.
    This is one of the longest pieces for the medium, and endurance is a factor for the double-reed instruments in the second and fourth movements. There is a balance of difficulty among the parts, although the first movement presents the greatest technical challenges. The contrapuntal nature of the last movement necessitates strict ensemble precision.

CONSTANT, MARIUS (1925-): France
*Trio (16:00). London: Chester (c1949)   (Grade VI)
    I. Allegro giocoso
    II. Scherzo (Allegro)
    III. Andante
    IV. Allegro ma non troppo

CONSTANT, MARIUS (1925–   ): France (Continued)
The most interesting aspect of this work is its varied harmonic style. Some passages are atonal while others tend to be more tonally based; the fourth movement even contains some bitonal sections. The melodic style is angular and chromatic, and the work's rhythmic vitality is a prominent element in the piece. It is dedicated to the René Daraux Trio d'Anches.
Due largely to the melodic contours and the lively rhythmic pace, the piece affords an opportunity for the woodwind players to display their agility and technical prowess. For example, the clarinet is featured in a long cadenza in the last movement. The French composers' penchant for writing for the oboe in its low register and for the bassoon in its altissimo register is also exemplified here. It should also be mentioned that some of the page turns in all three parts are virtually impossible to make while playing.

DANIELS, MABEL WHEELER (1878–   ): United States
    *Three Observations for Three Woodwinds, Op. 41 (7:24).
    New York: Carl Fischer (c1953)   (Grade IV-V)
        I. Ironic
        II. Canonic
        III. Tangonic

> Mabel Daniels has dealt discerningly with the instrumental
> combination, exploiting a number of its color possibilities,
> and has contrived a set of three pieces of medium difficulty
> that "conform to contest standards" .... The composer
> has endeavored to be as direct and intelligible as possible,
> yet sought to give her unoriginal ideas the appearance of the
> new. There is so much flitting around idiomatically that
> the piece sounds better on first hearing than it really is. [8]

The title of each movement suggests its character, and the prevailing mood is light. The work is dedicated to Louis Speyer and the Berkshire Woodwind Ensemble.
The performance of this piece is complicated somewhat by the irregular scale patterns and arpeggios and the intricate rhythms in the last movement. There is a balance of difficulty among the parts, and the principal technical requisite is flexibility, rather than speed. The score indicates that flute may be substituted for oboe.

DECADT, JEAN (1914–   ): Belgium
    *Trio (13:00). Brussels: Maurer (1950)   (Grade V-VI)
        I. Allegro
        II. Andante
        III. Scherzo

                    *   *   *

8. Persichetti, Vincent, Review in Notes 11:157 Dec 1953.

An austere and highly abstract character pervades all three movements of this work. Thick, imitative textures are employed almost exclusively in the first two movements, while all twelve chromatic notes are used freely in melodic material. Rhythmic motion is evident in almost every measure of the piece, and concerted rhythmic scoring is found only in the Scherzo.

Ensemble precision is complicated by the intricate rhythmic scoring and the persistent contrapuntal texture. The full range of all the instruments is utilized, and several extended low-register passages in oboe will require careful control. A low a is scored for oboe in the Scherzo -- possibly an oversight by the composer!

DEFOSSEZ, RENÉ (1905-   ): Belgium
  *Trio à anches (14:00). Brussels: CeBeDeM (1946)
                                                      (Grade V-VI)
    I.   Un peu large; Allegro moderato
    II. Lent, mais pas trop; Mouvemente de marche lente
    III. Allegro giocoso
Of particular interest in this work is the expressive quality of the melodic writing and the rhythmic vitality of the last movement. A plaintive oboe solo opens the second movement followed by a short solo clarinet passage and a slow march. Harmonic and melodic materials are derived from modal, pentatonic, and chromatic scales.

The opening measures of this trio are scored in octaves and are difficult to coordinate due to the changes in tempi and the awkward sixteenth-note passages. The key signature of the middle section of the second movement (four sharps) creates some difficult technical passages for all of the instruments. The concerted rhythmic style of the last movement demands very disciplined ensemble playing. Rapid staccato articulation and advanced technique are requisites throughout.

DELMOTTE, CAMILLE (1914-   ): Belgium
  *Trio (6:00). Brussels: Maurer (1947)   (Grade IV)
    I. Adagio
    II. Allegro moderato
The composer suggests two different instrumentations for this work: oboe, clarinet, and bassoon, or oboe, clarinet, and horn in F. Two different clarinet parts are included, one for use with bassoon, the other for use with horn. Parts for both versions are provided. With the exception of a few isolated passages in a concerted style in the second movement, the entire work is written in an imitative, contrapuntal fashion. Although key centers are occasionally implied in the individual lines, tonal organization is not apparent overall.

There are few serious problems involved in the performance of this rather short work. The independent character of the individual parts and the varied rhythms in the last movement should be a challenge to young players capable of handling moderate demands in technique and range.

DELVAUX, ALBERT (1913-   ): Belgium
*Trio (16:00). Brussels: CeBeDeM (1948)   (Grade IV-V)
   I. Allegro non troppo
   II. Burlesca
   III. Andante
   IV. Finale

This very melodious work features a variety of textures in an atonal idiom. The melodic writing maintains a cantabile character despite the prevailing atonality; the third movement is particularly noteworthy in this regard. The percussive use of dissonance and rhythmic vitality characterizes the last movement.

Most of the technical demands of this work are found in the last movement. The 5/4 meter throughout the third movement poses no serious ensemble problem since the tempo is not particularly fast.

DESPREZ, FERNAND (   ): Belgium
*Prélude et danse (5:45). Brussels: Brogneaux (c1950)
                                                        (Grade VI)
   I. Lent et espressif; Allegretto non troppo

This two-part work offers contrasts in texture, mood, and harmonic chromaticism. The opening Prelude is rhapsodic and very chromatic; the long melodies in oboe are accompanied by rapid arpeggio figures in the other instruments creating a thick, complicated texture. The Danse is less serious in character, more rhythmic, and in ternary form. The slow, descending motive that opens the work is recalled near the end; this is followed by a return of the animated pace that dominates the Danse.

The rubato style of the first section demands sensitive, mature players, and the rapid, accompaniment figuration in clarinet is very difficult. The fluctuating tempi, wide variety of rhythmic figures, and complex textures complicate ensemble precision. Much of the bassoon part is notated either in tenor clef or treble clef. Technical facility of the highest order is required in all three parts.

D'HOIR, JOSEPH (1929-   ): Belgium
*Variaties op "Een Kint Geboren in Bethlehem" (6:00).
Brussels: Maurer (1965)   (Grade IV)
   I. Inleiding adagio
      Variations: 1. Allegro moderato
               2. Allegro vivace
               3. Fantasia andante
               4. Allegro moderato
               5. Allegro
               6. Larghetto
               7. Allegro

After a brief introduction in clarinet and bassoon which suggests the opening motive of the main theme, the folk-like tune is stated in its entirety in oboe. Most of the variations that follow employ rather conventional variation techniques, such as imitation and changes of meter and tempi.

In the fourth variation an unembellished version of the melody in bassoon is accompanied by rhythmic figuration in oboe and clarinet.

Good high school players should be able to handle this piece very well. Technical and range demands are not advanced, but the many changes of tempo will require careful attention by younger players.

DOBROWOLSKI, ANDRZEJ (1921-   ): Poland
   *Trio (13:00). Cracow, Poland: Polskie Wydawnictwo Muzyczne (1956)
                                               (Grade V-VI)

     I. Allegro vivo
    II. Adagio
   III. Vivo

Dobrowolski's most frequently used texture is that of pairing two instruments in an accompanimental part against a rhythmically contrasting line. All three movements are multimetric, chromatic, and employ closed forms. A fugato serves as the contrasting "B" section of the three-part first movement. The emphasis in the fast movements is upon high-spirited rhythm, while the Adagio is more expressive and harmonically tense.

An f-sharp^3 is written for oboe in the first movement, while the bassoonist must cope with frequent tenor-range passages and a d-flat^2 in the first movement. The last movement offers the greatest challenge in technical facility and ensemble precision; its thematic material is highly chromatic, disjunct, and fast-paced. Only a full score is published for this work; no individual parts are printed.

DONDEYNE, DÉSIRÉ (1921-   ): France
   Suite d'airs populaires (14:30). Paris: Editions Musicales
   Transatlantiques (c1962)   (Grade V)

      I. Introduction et l'alouette (Allegro)
     II. Quand je suis parti de la Rochelle (Andante)
    III. Le chant de Jeanne (Allegro)
    IV. Le chant des Rameurs (Mouvemente de barcarolle)
     V. Le furet (Lent; Allegretto)
    VI. Petite valse
   VII. Invitation a la danse (Andantino)
  VIII. Le petite navire sur l'o helle (Allegretto)
    IX. Fugue sur la route de Dijon (Allegro)
     X. Bouquet final (Allegro)

This suite of short movements is based on popular, French folk songs, and tonal and modal elements are combined in the melody and harmony. Rhythms are quite simple, and the texture is uncomplicated and homophonic. Thematic material from the first movement is incorporated into the Bouquet final. A light, unpretentious mood prevails throughout the work.

A trio programming this work may want to consider doing only selected movements due to the number of movements in the work and the lack of contrast among them. Many passages are written in octaves and unisons, and careful attention must be paid to intonation. A reasonably advanced technique is required in all parts, and the oboe range is extended near its upper limits.

DUBOIS, PIERRE MAX (1930-   ): France
    *Trio d'anches (9:15). Paris: Leduc (c1958)   (Grade V)
        I. Humoresque (Allegro)
        II. Ritournelle (Andantino)
        III. Aubade (Scherzando)
Typical of many Paris Conservatory composers of the twentieth century,
Dubois writes in a light and humorous style. Chromatic scales, unexpected
harmonic relationships, and lively rhythms abound. The last movement
could be regarded as a nearly perfect example of scherzo writing prevalent
in many woodwind pieces by French composers.

    The technical requirements for works of this genre include agile facility
and rapid, light articulation. Although this work is no exception, Dubois does
write idiomatically for the instruments, and there are few awkward passages.
Endurance is of concern to the oboist and bassoonist in the second movement
where virtually no rests are provided. Except for a few instances of e^3 and
f-sharp^3 in oboe, the range demands are not severe. There are virtually
impossible page turns in the first movement of the oboe and clarinet parts.

DUIJCK, GUY (1927-   ): Belgium
    *Divertissement, Op. 14 (8:00). Brussels: Maurer (1956)
                                                        (Grade IV-V)
        I. Prelude (Moderato)
        II. Allegretto
        III. Elegie (Grave)
        IV. Scherzo
What sets this work apart from most other contemporary Belgian
composers' trios is the clear-cut, tonal harmonic idiom. Conventional key
signatures are employed, and the melodic structure is based primarily on
scale and triad material. However, both harmonic and melodic chromaticism
occur frequently, particularly between cadence points. The fast movements
are especially cheerful and high-spirited, while the other movements are more
cantabile and somewhat more contrapuntal. The oboe is featured throughout
most of the Elegie.

    The Scherzo presents the most serious performance problems in the work
with its rapid 3/8 meter and awkward sixteenth-note passages across the
register break for clarinet. With the exception of the latter, demands in
range and technical facility are not too severe.

EISMA, WILL (1929-   ): Holland
    *Affairs III (6:05). Amsterdam: Donemus (1965)   (Grade VI)
    This is the most 'avant-garde' of all of the works surveyed in this
study. The composer's notes in the score, the notation, and the style must
be studied carefully for a successful performance. Thematic material ranges
from rapid, disjunct patterns to sustained pitches. A great deal of emphasis
is placed on instrumental timbre and harmonic color. All of the materials
are carefully controlled, and there are no aleatoric passages.

The most difficult problems in performing this work are those of deciphering its notation and organizing it in ensemble. The passages marked "presto possibile" require virtuoso players with agile technical facility, wide range, and flexibility.

ESCHER, RUDOLF (1912-   ): Holland
  *Trio d'anches, Op. 4 (14:00). Amsterdam: Donemus (1946)
                                                    (Grade VI)
      I. Pastorale; Rondeau; Fugue; Pastorale
  "Other important chamber works by Escher include a remarkable Wind Trio (oboe, clarinet, and bassoon) . . . . Much of the music is extremely fragile and delicate in texture, with every note weighed almost as in Webern."[9] This is one of the most unusual works for the medium, and much of its originality centers about the scoring in the multi-sectional Rondeau movement. Most of this part of the piece consists of lengthy solo passages of a lyric nature stated alternately in oboe and clarinet. This section is introduced and concluded with a lively fugato in all three instruments. The first and last movements are very rhapsodic and similar in rhythmic style. The harmony is chromatic, mildly dissonant, and, at times, coloristic. Only in the Fugue are there tonal implications.
  From the point of view of ensemble playing, this is one of the most difficult works to put together, especially in the outer movements. The altissimo register of all three instruments is frequently utilized, and, in one instance in the Rondeau, there is a sustained f^3 for the oboe. The movements are to be performed 'attacca'.

EWERS, JÜRGEN (1937-   ): Germany
  Trio, Op. 2 (9:30). Wien, Germany: Krenn (1961)   (Grade V)
      I.   Marcia
      II. Molto sostenuto
      III. Allegretto scherzando
  The opening march is in a three-part form with the outer sections in 5/4 meter and the middle section in 4/4 meter. Two themes are prominent in the movement: one based on a descending chromatic scale and the other with frequent fourths and fifths. The second movement is contrapuntal and melodically angular. A more tonal harmonic organization is evident in the spirited last movement. The oboe is very prominent in much of the work.
  The scoring for oboe and bassoon demands a particularly wide range, and endurance is a factor for all three instruments in the middle movement. Technical requirements are somewhat advanced, but there should be little difficulty in ensemble rhythmic precision.

                    *   *   *

  9. Cobbett, op. cit., p. 80.

                            31

FAVRE, GEORGES (1905-   ): France
    *Gouaches-Suite (9:00). Paris: Durand (c1957)   (Grade VI)
        I. Pastorale
        II. Intermède
        III. Grave
        IV. Danse

Favre places most of the emphasis on the melodic element, favoring a highly tuneful and rhythmically varied style. The harmonic idiom is quite chromatic and makes use of all twelve chromatic notes. As a result, most passages are without a clear tonal center. The title of each movement suggests its prevailing mood or character.

Technical requirements are very demanding in all three parts, and the wide-ranging melodies exploit the full compass of the instruments. Rhythmic ensemble is complicated by the presence of multimeters and groupings of irregular rhythmic patterns (5-notes, 7-notes, etc.).

FELDERHOF, JAN (1907-   ): Holland
    *Thema met variaties (5:30). Amsterdam: Donemus (1943)
                                                                    (Grade V)
        I. Andante
            Variations: 1. Doppio movimento
                         2. Molto tranquillo
                         3. Vivace
                         4. Allegretto con moto
                         5. Moderato
                         6. Giocoso

The six, short variations in this little piece are based on a folk-like theme in the phrygian mode presented plaintively in oboe at the beginning. For the most part, the variations are of the melodic type coupled with changes in tempo, texture, and rhythmic pace. The oboe is featured in variations one and three. The clarinet is prominent in variation four in a chromatic, arpeggiated accompaniment to an augmented statement of the theme in oboe and bassoon. All of the instruments are on an equal basis in the other sections of the work.

Demands in facility are made on the oboe in variation three and on the clarinet in variation four. Ensemble precision is complicated somewhat by the contrapuntal texture in the last two variations. There is a sustained b^3 for clarinet near the end of the work, and the altissimo register of the bassoon is frequently used. The score, reproduced from the composer's manuscript, is not always easy to read.

    *Rondo (5:30). Amsterdam: Donemus (1960)   (Grade V)
This one-movement work is marked "Tempo di Valzer (rubato), " and is characterized by its chromatic harmonic idiom and constantly changing tempi. A flowing, cantabile theme undergoes considerable elaboration as the work unfolds. Each recurrence of the rondo theme is different from the one preceding it, and the form is more of a through-composed type than a rondo. The rhythmic style is as varied as the treatment of the theme, with an interesting musical balance among the instruments.

32

Except for occasional passages of animated accompanying figures, technical requirements are not severe. On the other hand, an ensemble will find the work difficult to put together due to the many subtle changes in tempo and texture. A few measures of the bassoon part are scored in the instrument's extreme altissimo register.

FERROUD, PIERRE-OCTAVE (1900-1936): France
  *Trio en mi (9:50). Paris: Durand (1933)   (Grade V-VI)
      I. Allegro moderato
     II. Allegretto grazioso
    III. Quasi presto
Ferroud uses a highly chromatic harmonic idiom that rarely delineates the tonalities suggested by the key signatures. The rhythms are varied, and multimeters are frequent. Duets for oboe and clarinet, often in thirds and sixths, are frequent, and the oboe dominates in the last two movements.

Although the bassoon part is the least prominent of the three instruments, it is the most difficult to play. Its accompanimental part is complicated by the wide range and angular figures scored for it. Ensemble rhythmic precision is difficult in the first movement. Intonation could be problematic at the beginning of the last movement where several measures are written in octaves. Clarinet in A is required throughout.

FLÉGIER, ANGE (1846-1927): France
  *Concert Suite (13:00). Paris: Gallet (1897), Chicago: Rubank (c1941)
                                                   (Grade V-VI)
      I. Allegro agitato
     II. Andante
    III. Intermezzo (Allegro scherzando)
     IV. Finale

> It is not impossible, however, within a limited sphere, to obtain a charming effect from a trio of sufficiently evenly-matched wind instruments such as an oboe, a clarinet, and a bassoon, the three-part basis being well adapted to show off, severally, the different values of each factor in the ensemble. In Flégier's Trio in B minor this very combination is treated with such a sure touch that the result is delightful. We hear in this passage from the "Intermezzo," for instance, the oboe in its playful mood, the bassoon on its most delicate 'staccato' notes, and the clarinet lending its rich expressive tone to the more smoothly written middle voice which binds the whole together.... But Flégier gives as much variety as possible, always considers the special aptitudes of the separate instruments, and shows due regard for the necessity of brevity in each of the four movements.[10]

                    *   *   *

10. Dunhill, T. F., Chamber Music, pp. 272-4.

FLÉGIER, ANGE (1846-1927): France (Continued)
The original edition of this work, published by Gallet, is titled T r i o.
It is in B minor and calls for clarinet in A throughout. Although separate
parts were available at one time, only the full score is now published. The
score bears a dedication to Jules Massenet. The Rubank edition, revised by
Himie Voxman, is little more than a transposition of the original up one-half
step to C minor, and it calls for clarinet in B-flat throughout. On the basis
of the writer's research on works in print for the reed trio, this work is the
earliest composed for the medium that is still available. This conclusion is
also shared by Himie Voxman.[11] Its style is reminiscent of late nineteenth-
century French overtures, such as those of Massenet, and its appeal is
centered around its graceful melodies and coloratura instrumental writing.

This florid melodic style is particularly evident in the clarinet part in the
first movement, while all of the instruments reveal their respective virtuoso
capabilities in the last movement where the rapid articulation is very demanding.
For the bassoonist, the Gallet edition is easier to read since its use of tenor
clef in several passages eliminates many leger lines in tenor range. The
Rubank edition uses bass clef throughout.

FONTYN, JACQUELINE (1930-   ): Belgium
*Sept petites pièces (9:00). Brussels: CeBeDeM (1956)
(Grade V)
    I. Allegretto grazioso
   II. Scherzando
  III. Andantino
  IV. Risoluto
   V. Lento
  VI. Moderato
 VII. Allegro moderato

Fontyn combines a variety of diverse elements in these short pieces.
The third piece opens with a chant-like theme in clarinet and bassoon, while
the following movement is light and witty. The fifth movement is quite
rhapsodic and features each instrument in a short cadenza. A mixture of
modal, tonal, and atonal influences are evident in the harmonic and melodic
materials throughout the work.

The third and seventh movements present the most difficult ensemble
problem due to the multimeters and rhythmic intricacies. Technical facility
is demanded in all of the instruments in the second movement, and the clarinet
part is particularly difficult in the last movement.

FORET, FÉLICIEN (   ): France
*Suite (7:45). Paris: Costallat (c1953)   (Grade IV-V)
   I. Prélude
  II. Pastorale
 III. Danse

               *   *   *

11. Personal letter written by Himie Voxman to the writer on April 8, 1969.

34

The most striking feature of this work is the lyric, cantabile quality that pervades all three movements. The melodic material is shared equally by all instruments with the bassoon being unusually prominent. Rhythms are uncomplicated and straightforward, and the tonal harmonic idiom uses chromatic chords frequently. The work is dedicated to the Trio d'Anches de Paris.

Although the facility required of the players is not particularly advanced, the extended passages of altissimo-register playing demand considerable control from all three players. Some awkward passages for clarinet could have been simplified by writing for the clarinet in A, rather than the B-flat.

FRANÇAIX, JEAN (1912-   ): France
*Divertissement (9:45). Mainz, Germany: Schott (c1954)
(Grade VI)

I. Prélude
II. Allegretto assai   **1710674**
III. Elégie
IV. Scherzo

> The delightful little piece of Françaix will surprise no one, but is sure to please all who find his idiom congenial. It is certainly one of his lighter works, which are unfortunately the only ones familiar to many. The four movements ... while formally straightforward, are full of the composer's very personal charm and whimsy. The Elégie especially has a hushed, haunting atmosphere, reminiscent of the slow movement of Ravel's Concerto in G, and the entire work is perfectly conceived for the three winds. [12]

This work is dedicated to the André Dupont Trio and demands virtuoso performances from all three instrumentalists. Although the most critical performance problem is rhythmic precision, the technical and range requirements are, indeed, severe.

FRANCK, MAURICE (1897-   ): France
Trio (6:30). Paris: Selmer (c1937)   (Grade IV)
I. Pastorale
II. Scherzo
III. Andante
IV. Final

Very light in character, Franck's first work for the medium is characterized by a rich and colorful harmonic style with frequent parallel harmonic motion. Emphasis is also placed on a cantabile melodic style and lively rhythms. The work is dedicated to the Trio d'Anches de Paris.

*   *   *

12. Rosenthal, L., Review in Notes 12:641 Sept 1955.

FRANCK, MAURICE (1897-   ): France (Continued)
The oboe is the most prominent instrument throughout. Technical
demands are only moderately advanced, but light, fast articulation is of
utmost importance in the second and fourth movements. Some passages in
the second movement are particularly intricate in the clarinet part involving
the left hand and rapid changes of register.

Deuxième trio d'anches (12:45). Paris: Editions Musicales
Transatlantiques (c1960)   (Grade V-VI)
    I.   Adagio; Allegretto
   II. Allegro vivace
  III. Andantino
  IV. Lent; Allegro

Franck maintains a light character through the use of transparent,
homophonic textures and lively rhythms. The themes are derived mainly
from chromatic scales and modes. The bassoon is particularly important
with solo passages or prominent melodic material in virtually every movement. A cantabile bassoon line in the third movement is accompanied by a
highly rhythmic duet by oboe and clarinet.

The most difficult of the three parts is the oboe because of its arpeggio
and scale passages in the altissimo register. The greatest ensemble problem
is the duet by oboe and clarinet mentioned above, which is written in 64th-notes,
and is thus difficult to coordinate with the bassoon part. There are also page
turns in all the parts that are virtually impossible to make while playing.

GALLON, NOËL (1891-1957): France
*Suite en trio (12:00). Paris: Selmer (c1933)   (Grade IV-V)
    I.   Allemande
   II. Fugue
  III. Sarabande
  IV. Tambourin

Although the prevailing character of this suite is light, Gallon uses a
variety of textures, harmonies, and melodies based on modes and major-
minor scales. He frequently pairs the oboe and clarinet in thirds, fourths,
and fifths, and all of the instruments share in the melodies. The inner two
movements are more contrapuntal than the outer movements.

The performance problems are typical of many French works for the medium:
light, rapid articulation, wide range, and advanced technical facility. Some
passages for bassoon are notated in treble clef. The last movement seems
virtually unplayable at the composer's suggested metronome marking.

GERAEDTS, JAAP (1924-   ): Holland
*Divertimento No. 1 (10:00). Amsterdam: Donemus (1943)
                                                      (Grade V-VI)
    I.   Intrada (Allegro-tempo di marcia)
   II. Intermezzo (Lento)
  III. Rondo (Allegro vivace)

The most striking aspect of this work is the Intermezzo, its rhapsodic opening section featuring the oboe and clarinet. Afterwards, the movement settles into a lyric duet in oboe and bassoon accompanied by an animated clarinet part that is woven into the rest of the movement. The outer movements are light in character and highly rhythmic. Most of the themes are derived from triads, but the harmonic idiom is not tonal. The level of dissonance is rather high, and many chords are built in seconds and fourths.

There is a balance of both musical interest and difficulty among the parts, with the middle movement presenting the most difficulty in ensemble precision. Technical requirements are somewhat advanced, and the articulation indicated throughout most of the Rondo is difficult to execute. An extended passage in octaves which requires careful attention to intonation closes the work.

*Divertimento No. 2 (12:00). Amsterdam: Donemus (1946)

(Grade V)

    I. Ouverture (Allegro con spirito)
    II. Pastorale; Musette
    III. Burlesca (Giocoso, tempo vivace)
    IV. Finale (Alla marcia)

The most obvious elements of this work are its spirited rhythm and a somewhat dissonant, chromatic harmony. Modulations are frequent and abrupt, often within the span of a phrase. A poignant oboe line in the Pastorale is accompanied by a dissonant duet in clarinet and bassoon. The Burlesca is in a fast triple meter, and there is a witty use of dissonance. The clarinet is prominent in the last movement, and a brilliant, contrapuntal coda closes the work.

The performance problems in this work are its technical demands, ensemble precision, wide range in bassoon, and dynamic control; one passage in the second movement is marked "ppp possible."

GILTAY, BEREND (1910-   ): Holland
    *Sonata à tre (13:00). Amsterdam: Donemus (1953)   (Grade V-VI)
      I. Allegro-spiritoso
      II. Thema con variazioni
      III. Rondo-Allegro

Employing a somewhat complex, chromatic harmonic idiom, Giltay fashions a texture in which short motives, derived from thematic material stated at the beginning of the movements, are elaborated and developed as the music unfolds. The theme in the middle movement is first stated in oboe; it is subsequently reworked in three variations, each featuring a different instrument. The last variation is particularly rhapsodic for the oboe.

The most critical problem in performing this work is ensemble precision which is complicated by multimeters and the independent character of each part; the first movement and the third variation of the second movement are the most difficult in this respect. Other difficulties are brought about by the unexpected accidentals, non-idiomatic finger combinations, and disjunct melodic contours.

GOLESTAN, STAN (1872-1956): Rumania; France
*Petite suite bucolique (9:00). Paris: Durand (c1953)
(Grade V-VI)

I. Humoresque
II. Lamento
III. Jeux

All three movements are in a somewhat free, ternary form. A cyclic feature occurs near the end of the work where melodic material from the Humoresque is recalled. The oboe is prominent in the last movement with a quasi-oriental theme in which melodic augmented seconds abound. The thematic material, usually of a lyric, expressive nature, is often presented in duets. The harmonic idiom is chromatic, and key centers are rarely delineated until the end of sections or movements.

The first two movements have constantly fluctuating tempi within them. The closing measures of the work, written in octaves, are technically awkward. There is a balance of difficulty among the parts, but the oboe and clarinet share most of the important melodic material.

GOUÉ, EMILE (1904-1946): France
*Trois pièces: bagatelle, mélopée, scherzo (8:00).
Paris: Editions du Magasin Musical Pierre Schneider (c1939)
(Grade V)

I. Bagatelle
II. Mélopée
III. Scherzo

Featuring the oboe and clarinet prominently, these short, light pieces combine a mixture of tonal and modal harmonies, a variety of scale materials, and an animated rhythmic style. All three movements are cast in a loose three-part form. The ten-measure theme that opens the Mélopée in oboe, and later in clarinet, is particularly striking for its cantabile character. The work is dedicated to the Trio d'Anches de Paris.

A serious problem for the clarinetist in this work is the fact that the B-flat clarinet is called for in the outer movements, while the clarinet in A is specified in the slow movement. Transferring to the clarinet in A for the middle movement could present a problem in tuning. The first movement is notated in five flats (concert key) and offers some challenges in both reading and fingering for the double-reed instruments.

GOULD, ELIZABETH (1904-): United States
*Disciplines (4:35). Philadelphia: Elkan-Vogel (c1964)
(Grade IV-V)

This composition, an exercise in economy of means, consists of a melody limited to the common range of the three instruments, followed by three variations and a conclusion. All parts are constructed on a series of seven scales or modes ranging from the darkest to the brightest.

At the same time other means such as rhythm and pitch are used to increase the intensity of the music to a point just preceding the conclusion. This was an attempt to make music as meaningful and interesting as possible while strictly observing a number of limitations. [13]

Although the composer mentions in her note in the score that the melody is "limited to the common range of the three instruments," the tessitura for the bassoon is rather high throughout, and there is considerable use of the oboe in its extreme low register. Intonation is problematic in the opening measures due to an extended passage written in octaves involving all three instruments. A variety of textures is employed throughout, and the unusual modal scale patterns add to the level of difficulty.

GRABNER, HERMANN (1886-   ): Austria
  Trio (15:00). Leipzig: Kistner and Siegel (1951)   (Grade V-VI)
    I.   Straff und energisch bewegt
    II. Ruhig, und aus drucksvoll
    III. Rasch, wuchtig
    IV. Sehr lebhaft, burlesk

Most of the thematic material of the first movement is derived from the opening, multimetric theme. The prevailing mood throughout the work is light and witty. The harmonic idiom is tonal with frequent modulations. Chromaticism is an important factor in the melodies. The clarinet and oboe are very prominent in the third movement, but, for the most part, there is a balance of interest among the parts.

Grabner's style requires players with a solid technique, wide dynamic range, and flexibility. Rhythms are complex, and several passages scored in octaves demand careful attention to intonation. There are also many measures that use the altissimo register of the oboe.

GRIEND, KOOS van de (1905-1950): Holland
  *Trio (4:40). Amsterdam: Donemus (1929)   (Grade V-VI)
    I.   Moderato
    II. Andante
    III. Presto

Griend maintains a non-tonal approach in each movement, with texture and rhythm being the principal elements of contrast from movement to movement. The first is angular in melodic design and somewhat contrapuntal. Imitation and a more cantabile mood characterize the middle movement, while the Presto features lively, syncopated rhythms and irregular arpeggio and scale patterns.

The last movement is the most difficult technically, its accelerated rhythmic pace also creating the work's most demanding ensemble challenge. There is a balance of interest and difficulty among the three parts.

*   *   *

13. Composer's remarks on the cover of the full score.

d'HARCOURT, MARGUERITE BÉCLARD (1884-   ): France
     Rapsodie Péruvienne (12:00). Paris: Lemoine (1945)
                                                  (Grade V)
     I.   Pastorale dans les Andes (Modéré, sans trainer)
     II. Wayno (Danse pour la récolte du mais)
     III. Yaravi (Chant d'amour)
     IV. Katchampa (Danse guerrière)
Marguerite d'Harcourt is a French composer and musicologist and, like
her husband, is an authority on the Indian music of Peru. The melodic
material in this suite is based on themes from that music. The style of each
movement follows closely the programmatic connotations of the titles, or
subtitles. Pentatonic scales are an important factor in many of the themes.
Among the most noteworthy sections of this unusual work for the medium are
the clarinet and bassoon duet that opens the piece, the poignant third
movement, and the gruff, strident Katchampa. It is dedicated to the
Rene Daraux Trio d'Anches.
     The marked contrast in character from movement to movement requires
players with some degree of musical maturity. Close attention must be paid
to ensemble rhythmic precision, and requirements in technical facility are
advanced.

HERMANS, NICO J. (1919-   ): Holland
     *Divertimento Piccolo, Op. 2 (6:00). Amsterdam: Donemus (1948)
                                                  (Grade IV-V)
     I.   Introduktion
     II. Rondino
These two short movements are quite dissimilar in mood and style. The
first is very chromatic, somewhat rhapsodic, strikingly poignant, and, at
times, sharply dissonant. The Rondino is cheerful, rhythmic, and more
tonally organized. Brackets are employed as a notational device to frame
important thematic material.
     Performance problems include altissimo-register playing in bassoon,
ensemble rhythmic precision in the last movement, and intonation in angular
melodic passages scored in unisons and octaves. There are also very awkward
tremolos across the register break for clarinet in the first movement.

HOFFER, PAUL (1895-1949): Germany
     *Kleine Suite (6:15). Hamburg: Sikorski (1944)   (Grade III-IV)
     I.   Moderato
     II. Allegro
     III. Adagio
     IV. Allegretto
     V.   Alla marcia
This short set of pieces serves as good ensemble material for younger
players, particularly with regard to developing correct concepts of balance
and projection. Its style is unpretentious and straightforward with the

emphasis upon melodic, legato writing for all three instruments. Multimeters are used in the third movement, but the same beat unit is employed in each meter which makes for little or no rhythmic ensemble problem.

Technical and range demands are very minimal, and most junior and senior high school players should find this work well within their command. Due to a printing error all editorial markings have been omitted from the bassoon part. Older and more musically sophisticated players may find Hoffer's style dull and pedantic.

*Thema mit Variationen (4:30). Hamburg: Sikorski (1944)
(Grade III-IV)

Only in the formal organization is this work different from Hoffer's other work for the medium discussed above. In variation 5 of the clarinet part, measures 11 and 12 should be omitted as they are needless repetitions of measures 9 and 10; the player should play measure 10 and proceed to measure 13.

Except for more frequent use of the low register of the oboe in these variations, both of Hoffer's works are similar in degree of difficulty.

HOSKINS, WILLIAM (   ): United States
*Prelude and Fugue (4:45). New York: Composers Facsimile
Edition (c1955)   (Grade IV)
    I.   Prelude (Allegro moderato)
    II. Fugue (Molto moderato)
Both of the movements are contrapuntal and highly chromatic. Most of the Prelude is involved with the development of the opening theme, the rhythm of which undergoes considerable elaboration; the movement closes with a lengthy allargando passage in which the main theme is restated in oboe and clarinet accompanied by a sustained pedal point in the bassoon. The five-measure fugue subject is stated successively in oboe, clarinet, and bassoon. The texture is lightened during occasional duet episodes.

The score indicates that the work may also be performed by two clarinets and bassoon. Although Hoskin's note on the score states that transposed clarinet parts are available, only the full score is now published. Ensemble precision is the only serious performance problem. Much of the bassoon part is notated in tenor clef, but most of these passages are not in the tenor range.

IBERT, JACQUES (1890-1962): France
    Cinq pièces en trio (7:00). Paris: L'Oiseau-Lyre (1935)
(Grade IV-V)
    I.   Allegro vivo
    II. Andantino
    III. Allegro assai
    IV. Andante
    V.   Allegro quasi marziale

IBERT, JACQUES (1890-1962): France (Continued)

Very light in character, these very short pieces are similar in mood to Ibert's Trois pièces brèves for woodwind quintet and are dedicated to Fernand Oubradous and the Trio d'Anches de Paris. Combining features of impressionism and neo-classism, the work excels in its rhythmic vitality, melody, and coloristic, modal harmony.

The clarinet part is the most consistently demanding, but all three players are technically challenged in the last movement. The oboe and clarinet open the second movement with an extended duet.

IKONOMOW, BOYAN (1900-   ): Bulgaria; France
Trio en mi, Op. 14 (12:00). Paris: L'Oiseau-Lyre (1937)
(Grade V-VI)
 I. Allegro
 II. Andante
 III. Allegro molto
This work is one of several commissioned by Louise B. M. Dyer-Hanson during the 1930's. It reveals some folk song influence and the composer's interest in uneven meters. The entire last movement is in 7/8 meter. The harmonic idiom is tonal, but extremely chromatic. The melodic writing unfolds in a continuous, through-composed manner.

There are several awkward, if not impossible, page turns for the players to cope with as well as measure after measure of playing with no rests. The continuous 7/8 meter of the last movement would require a considerable amount of rehearsal time to perform it at the composer's suggested tempo of ♩ = 160. Clarinet in A is required throughout.

JOHANNES, JOHN (   ): Holland
*Introductie en fuga (2:25). Amsterdam: Donemus (1968)
(Grade IV-V)
 I. Introduzione (Lento)
 II. Fuga (Allegro con spirito)
This recent work is dedicated to the Rotterdam Windensemble, comprised of Cees van den Bergh, Gerrit Kryt, and Henk de Wit. Both movements are atonal and contrapuntal, and each begins with clarinet alone. Contrast is achieved by the more animated style of the Fuga.

The degree of difficulty of the last movement is directly related to the tempo established by the clarinet's statement of the fugue subject; the angular lines and multi-metric rhythms could be problematic at an extremely fast tempo. Demands in range and articulation are only moderate.

JONG, MARINUS de (1891-   ): Belgium
*Trio, Op. 126 (17:00). Brussels: CeBeDeM (1961)   (Grade V)
 I. Andante; Allegro risoluto
 II. Scherzo
 III. Finale-Rondo

This composer writes in a more conservative style than the other contemporary Belgian composers encountered in this study. His harmonic idiom is clearly tonal with the emphasis on tuneful, appealing melodic writing. His scoring is varied and interesting, and the three instruments are evenly balanced in difficulty and musical interest.

The clarinet part in the second movement could have been simplified had the composer scored it for clarinet in A rather than the B-flat clarinet; the five sharps in the key signature and the rhythmic pace combine to make for a complex part. There is a short cadenza for clarinet in the first movement up to a^3 in range. Most of the technical problems in the middle movement are determined by the tempo established by the trio.

JONGEN, LÉON (1885-   ): Belgium
  *Trio (16:00). San Antonio, Texas: Southern Music Co. (1937)
(Grade VI)
   I. Poco maestoso
   II. Vivace
   III. Andante; Allegro giocoso

Beginning with the opening measures, the prominence of the bassoon in this work is made quite evident. After it is joined by clarinet and oboe in imitative statements of the opening theme, the rhapsodic introduction is followed by a long-lined, lyric melody in oboe. It is based on motives from the bassoon introduction and accompanied by an animated duet in clarinet and bassoon. The introduction to the Allegro giocoso presents a chant-like theme in bassoon, and later in the clarinet. This leads to a bitonal march theme stated imitatively between oboe and clarinet.

Basically neo-romantic in style, this work requires not only technical flexibility, but flexibility with regard to tempo as well. The clarinet and bassoon parts offer the most severe technical challenges, and the writing, in general, exploits the instruments' full ranges and expressive capabilities. Considerable rehearsal time would be required to prepare this work for performance. Clarinet in A is needed throughout.

JUON, PAUL (1872-1940): Russia
  *Arabesken, Op. 73 (17:00). Berlin: Lienau (1940)
(Grade V-VI)
   I. Commodo
   II. Larghetto
   III. Allegretto (quasi Menuetto)
   IV. Vivo

Juon's trio represents one of the most flashy and brilliant works for the medium. The harmonies are tonal, and harmonic minor scales and melodic augmented seconds are frequent. The Larghetto is written primarily in a chordal, note-against-note style, while the last movement features a duet in thirds for clarinet and oboe throughout much of the movement.

JUON, PAUL (1872-1940): Russia (Continued)

Although there are challenges in technical facility for all three instruments, the writing is generally idiomatic and the work sounds more difficult than it really is. The full range of the instruments is exploited with occasional instances of c^2 for bassoon and f^3 for oboe. Precision in ensemble playing is complicated by the wide variety of rhythmic figures in each part. Intonation is problematic in the beginning of the last movement where the theme is stated in octaves involving all three instruments.

KELKEL, MANFRED (1929-   ): Germany
*Divertimento, Op. 3 (10:45). Paris: Ricordi (c1958)
(Grade V-VI)

   I.   Lento assai; Allegro giocoso
  II. Grotesque (Andante)
 III. Scherzo (Allegro)
 IV. Marcia funebre (Andante)
  V. Finale (Allegro giocoso)

After a short, highly expressive introduction featuring the bassoon in its altissimo range, the first movement proper begins with a rhythmic theme in bassoon answered imitatively in oboe and clarinet. After a section marked "Tempo di Valse, " the bassoon-dominated section returns and balances the ternary organization. Grotesque features the wide range of the bassoon, while the oboe and clarinet supply a tense, atmospheric background. The third and fifth movements are similar in spirit and rhythmic vitality, with the Marcia funebre exploiting the lyric, somber qualities of the oboe. There are few indications of strict tonal organization in Kelkel's dissonant, chromatic idiom. The work is dedicated to Darius Milhaud.

The work requires an excellent bassoonist due to the prominence and difficulty of the part. Only in the opening section and the third movement are there problems in ensemble precision.

KERSTERS, WILLEM (1929-   ): Belgium
*Berceuse en humoreske, Op. 8 (5:00). Brussels: Maurer (1956)
(Grade V)

  I. Berceuse (Andante)
 II. Humoreske (Moderato)

This short work is dedicated to the Brussels Wind Trio, and it is characterized by the chromatic, contrapuntal style of the Berceuse and the equally chromatic Humoreske. The latter is in ternary form, the outer sections of which are similar in texture and thematic material. The contrast in spirit between the two movements is implied in their respective titles.

Technical requirements are somewhat advanced, while ensemble precision is complicated by the independent character of the parts and the multimeters in the second movement. All the instruments share in presenting important melodic material, but the clarinet is particularly prominent in the second movement.

KLEIN, RICHARD RUDOLF (1921-   ): Germany
  *Serenade (12:00). Wilhelmshaven, Germany: O. H. Noetzel (c1960)
                                                              (Grade IV)
      I.   Alla marcia
      II. Scherzo
      III. Variationen
      IV. Andantino
      V.   Finale
  Klein achieves cohesion in this suite by recalling thematic material in
later movements that was stated in the early part of the work. These cyclic
themes are usually modified and rarely recur in their original form. For
instance, material from the middle section of the Scherzo serves as the basis
for the fourth movement at a slower tempo. Most harmonic and melodic
materials are derived from triads, but clear tonal relationships between
chords or keys are not evident. The variations of the third movement are of
the melodic type; a new melody is invented to the original scheme of harmony
and presented in a different instrument in each of the three variations.
  Except for a few altissimo-register passages for oboe, there are few technical problems in this work. The three parts go together easily in ensemble.

KOCSÁR, MIKLÓS (   ): Hungary
  *Divertimento (7:30). Budapest: Zeneműkiadó Vállalat (c1966)
                                                              (Grade IV-V)
      I.   Allegretto leggiero
      II. Calmo
      III. Vivo
  Kocsár combines atonality, multimeters, and a variety of textures in a
work with only isolated technical difficulties. The second movement, which
opens with an unaccompanied clarinet line, is contrapuntal; dynamically
speaking, it is one long crescendo and diminuendo. The last movement is
lively in mood, contrapuntal in texture, and cyclic in formal design; a section
marked Calmo occurs near the end recalling the character, if not the
thematic material, of the middle movement. Trills embellish the disjunct
melodic material very frequently in the outer movements.
  Most of the technical problems in this piece are encountered in the last
movement, and the degree of difficulty would be increased as the tempo is
accelerated. The main theme of the third movement is stated in unaccompanied
bassoon at the beginning, and, because of its tenor range, it requires expert
control by the player. In fact, all of the instruments make considerable use
of their upper ranges, and this, combined with awkward fingering combinations,
presents the most severe performance problem.

KOECHLIN, CHARLES (1867-1950): France
  *Trio d'anches (13:00). Paris: Meridian (c1957)   (Grade VI)
      I.   Grave et serein, presque adagio
      II. Allegro
      III. Andante très calme
      IV. Allegro très animé

KOECHLIN, CHARLES (1867-1950): France (Continued)

Exploiting the virtuoso potential of the reed instruments, Koechlin writes in a refined, austere, and disciplined style. The harmonic idiom is tonal, but very chromatic.

Extreme range is one of the most critical problems in performing this work. The oboe part is written with frequent use of f-sharp^3 and g^3, and the clarinet must cope with numerous measures with g-sharp^3 and a^3. The second movement features a long solo passage for bassoon at the beginning, and the following movement opens with an oboe solo.

KOETSIER, JAN (1911-   ): Holland

*Zes Bagatellen, Op. 16, No. 2 (6:00). Amsterdam: Donemus
(1937)   (Grade IV-V)
    I.   Allegro giocoso
   II. Larghetto
  III. Vivace
  IV. Poco adagio
   V. Allegro burlesca
  VI. Andante

These six, short abstract pieces feature a moderately dissonant harmonic style and the use of multimeters. Movements I, III, and V are light and rhythmic, while a more cantabile melodic style is present in the slow movements. The Larghetto is in a Siciliano rhythm, and the fourth movement features the bassoon and a brief technical flourish for clarinet. The closing piece is a chorale.

Although the entire work does not require virtuoso-calibre performers, isolated passages do demand rapid, staccato articulation and an agile technique. The oboe part in the Vivace is an example of such demands. Multimeters usually present problems in ensemble rhythmic precision, but the brevity of these pieces helps to minimize the difficulty.

KREISLER, ALEXANDER von (   ): Russia; United States

*Trio (7:30). San Antonio, Texas: Southern Music Co. (c1964)
(Grade IV-V)
    I.   Allegro
   II. Andante
  III. Tempo di valse

This composer studied with Glazunov, Liadov, Tcherepnin, and others at the St. Petersburg Conservatory, and after coming to the United States in 1928 he became affiliated with the Cincinnati Conservatory and later the University of Texas. His writing shows the influence of his early training and the Russian preference for rich harmonies and expressive melodic writing. Attention is given to formal balance in each movement, and the third movement is in a clear-cut ternary form. The habanera rhythm of the middle movement and the unexpected harmonic shifts in the waltz are noteworthy features of the work.

The score indicates that flute may be used in place of the oboe, although the scoring is much more idiomatic for the latter. All three movements require flexibility in technique and close attention in ensemble playing due to the frequent tempo changes within movements. Each instrument is treated soloistically from time to time, and a balance of interest is maintained among the parts.

LEGLEY, VICTOR (1915-   ): Belgium
   *Trio, Op. 11 (12:00). Brussels: CeBeDeM (1942)   (Grade VI)
      I. Allegretto grazioso
     II. Adagio
    III. Allegretto
    IV. Allegro moderato

Written in an abstract style, Legley has created a rhythmically complex and challenging work dedicated to the Trio d'Anches de Bruxelles. Multimeters are present throughout, and the rhythmic materials are extremely varied.

The most severe challenge facing a trio preparing this work is the rhythmic element. Ensemble precision is complicated greatly by the constantly changing meters and the wide variety of rhythmic figures. Each of the parts is usually independent of the other two, and the chromatic melodic style is difficult to read.

LESUR, DANIEL (1908-   ): France
   *Suite (13:00). Paris: L'Oiseau (1939)   (Grade VI)
      I. Monodie et beguine (Andante)
     II. Diaphonie (Gaiament)
    III. Berceuse (Andantino)
    IV. Scherzo (Presto brillante)

Lesur's style is characterized by an emphasis on angular, chromatic thematic materials, parallel chord progressions, heightened rhythmic pace, and a high level of dissonance. Multimeters are used in the first movement; the work closes with a double cadenza for clarinet and bassoon.

The composer is principally an organist and pianist, and his lack of familiarity with wind instruments is evident in the demands he places upon them in this work. For instance, in the last movement either the metronome marking given by the composer or the articulation in the clarinet part would need to be altered as it is unplayable as written. Few clarinetists are able to articulate 16th-notes at $\flat = 84$ in 3/8 meter for the extended time required in the Scherzo. Another case in point is the numerous use of non-idiomatic, wide, descending leaps in the double-reed instruments. Clarinet in A is required throughout.

LEWIN, GORDON (   ): England
   Scherzola (3:30). London: Boosey and Hawkes (c1959) (Grade IV-V)

This short, one-movement piece combines humor, jazz, and an accelerated rhythmic pace. The harmonic-melodic style is tonal, and the triple meter is often punctuated with syncopations and unexpected cross rhythms.

47

LEWIN, GORDON (   ): England (Continued)
The clarinet part is somewhat more prominent and difficult than the
other instruments, although all are featured from time to time. A light,
fluent technique and rapid staccato are required, as well as strict rhythmic
precision in ensemble. This work should serve well as an encore selection.

MAEGAARD, JAN (1926-   ): Denmark
*Trio (8:00). Copenhagen: Dania (1950)   (Grade V-VI)
    I. Allegro moderato; Andante, un poco inquieto; Allegro simplice
This one-movement work is divided into three contrasting sections. "The
toccata-like variations in the middle of the trio are contrasted by the vivacious
character and more direct expression of the first and third movements."14
A lengthy, brilliant cadenza for clarinet opens and closes the Andante, un
poco inquieto and reveals the composer's predilection for the fourth as a
melodic interval. For the most part, the texture is contrapuntal in the
outer movements, and the prevailing harmonic idiom is very chromatic.

    The Grade VI level of difficulty applies to the clarinet part, since the
other parts are somewhat less difficult. The independent character of each
instrument's line makes ensemble precision more complicated, while the
chromatic melodic style makes for added complexity in reading. Clarinet
in A is called for throughout.

MAESSEN, ANTOON (1919-   ): Holland
*Cassation (10:00). Amsterdam: Donemus (1958)   (Grade IV-V)
    I. Intrada (Allegro energico)
    II. Notturno (Tranquillo)
    III. Capriccio (Scherzando)
    IV. Aria (Andantino)
    V. Burla (Allegretto)
    VI. Menuet
    VII. Tarantella (Vivace)
Each of the seven movements is quite short and based upon a melodic idea
appropriate to the title of the movement. For instance, the opening Intrada
uses dotted figures to effect a fanfare style, while the Aria is written in a
Siciliano rhythm. A frequently employed texture is that of an imitative duet
accompanied by the third instrument playing a different, less important part.
The harmonic and melodic writing uses all chromatic pitches very freely, and
polytonality is evident in certain passages. Most of the movements establish
F or C at the end of each as a type of harmonic focal point, but it would be
difficult to describe the style as tonal.

    Ensemble rhythmic coordination is difficult in the third movement; the
three parts are independent of each other throughout much of the work.
Demands in range and technique are only moderately advanced and well
within the capabilities of good high school players.

*   *   *

14. Larsen, Knud, ed., The Society for Publishing Danish
Music, p. 43.

48

MANIET, RENÉ (1920-   ): Belgium

*Concert d'anches (8:00). Brussels: Maurer (1964)   (Grade V-VI)
 I. Allegro
 II. Adagio
 III. Valse Viennoise (Moderato)
 IV. Scherzo

Similar in many respects to his earlier work for the medium discussed below, the emphasis here is upon brilliance and rhythmic vivacity. Melodic and harmonic materials are extremely varied, and tonal implications are only fleetingly apparent. The rhapsodic Adagio features the clarinet and bassoon prominently, and all three instruments share in the stylized melodies of the third movement.

This work requires three expert players due to its rhythmic pace, wide-ranging chromatic lines, and ensemble intricacies. There is a balance of difficulty and interest among the parts.

*Trio d'anches (4:30). Brussels: Maurer (c1959)   (Grade III-IV)
 I. Allegro moderato
 II. Andante
 III. Allegro

This brilliant little piece exploits the technical facility of the three instrumentalists. It is light in character and rhythmically animated, but not without its stylistic complexities. Multimeters are present in every movement, and melodies are derived from a variety of scale and arpeggio patterns. Chromatic scales and augmented triads are important elements in much of the thematic material. Textures are thin, homophonic, and only occasionally imitative.

The flexibility mentioned above requires three players with fluent technique. Ensemble rhythmic precision is problematic in the fast movements. The Andante is much simpler than the outer movement, and the Grade III applies to the middle movement only.

*Trio d'anches No. 2 (8:30). Brussels: Maurer (1960)
                                                                                (Grade V)

 I. Allegro moderato
 II. Quasi lento
 III. Allegretto
 IV. Allegro

Maniet shows a consistency of style in his three works for the reed trio medium. As in the other pieces discussed above, lively tempi, chromatic themes, and varied harmonic sonorities all abound. Quartal harmonies are particularly frequent in the second movement. A brief transition serves to connect the last two movements.

The subdivided meter and other rhythmic intricacies of the atmospheric slow movement are difficult to coordinate within the ensemble. Technical demands are challenging, but not severe. The clarinet part could have been greatly simplified had the composer scored it for clarinet in A instead of clarinet in B-flat.

MAROS, RUDOLF (1917-   ): Hungary
   Serenade (9:00). Budapest: Zeneműkiadó Vállalat (1951)
                                                    (Grade IV-V)
   I.   Allegro moderato
   II. Adagio
   III. Allegro molto
Multimeters are used throughout, but they are particularly frequent in
the second movement. The harmonic idiom constantly shifts between major
and minor. The middle movement is quite rhapsodic in character, and its
melodic construction indicates a possible folk influence. Maros emphasizes
the melodic and rhythmic elements of the work.

   The second movement presents numerous performance problems due to
the predominance of multimeters and the rubato character of the clarinet
part. Light articulation and expert technique are required by all three
players, but the clarinet part is somewhat more difficult in the final two
movements. There is also frequent altissimo-register playing for bassoon.
Players will need to check their respective parts for minor printing errors
too numerous to list here.

MARTELLI, HENRI (1895-   ): France
   *Trio, Op. 45 (15:00). Paris: Costallat (1938)   (Grade V-VI)
   I.   Allegro quasi moderato
   II. Molto lento
   III. Allegretto grazioso
This work is dedicated to Fernand Oubradous, bassoonist with the Trio
d'Anches de Paris, and it is not surprising that it is primarily a
display piece for bassoon, which is featured prominently in each movement.
The harmonic style is chromatic, and modulations are abrupt and frequent.
There is also pronounced rhythmic activity in all three movements. Brackets
are used here, as they are in several other French works under study, to
frame important melodic material.

   Besides the advanced technical facility required, the ensemble problem of
coordinating the fragmentary melodic ideas in all three parts is a critical one.
Martelli does not employ the extreme ranges of the instruments, and, in that respect,
the work is somewhat less challenging than other works of such advanced calibre.

MARTINON, JEAN (1910-   ): France
   *Sonatine No. 4, Op. 26, No. 1 (12:45). Paris: Costallat (1940)
                                                    (Grade V-VI)
   I.   Vivace
   II. Andante
   III. Vivace
This well-known conductor-composer was a student of the French neo-
classicist, Albert Roussel, and this trio clearly shows the influence of his
teacher. Emphasis is placed on clarity of form and color, both harmonic
and instrumental. Equal interest is maintained in all the parts, and a light,
cheerful mood is sustained throughout. The work is dedicated to the André
Dupont Trio d'Anches.

50

The wide variety of rhythmic figures and the rhythmically independent character of each of the instrumental parts create a complex ensemble problem in the two inner movements, but the players are aided, to a large degree, by the thoughtful printing of two parts in score form during the most intricate passages. Technical facility of a high order is required of the oboist and clarinetist, while the bassoon writing demands control of the entire range of the instrument. A curious printing arrangement finds the first and last pages of the bassoon part on the inner pages of the title cover.

MARTINU, BOHUSLAV (1890-1959): Czechoslovakia
*Quatre madrigaux (18:30). Paris: Eschig (1937)

(Grade VI)

    I. Allegro moderato
    II. Lento
    III. Poco allegretto
    IV. Poco allegro

Rhythmic vivacity and cantabile melodic writing are the most prominent elements of these madrigals. Most melodic and harmonic materials are derived from triads, but the use of these materials is extremely varied. Multimeters and cross rhythms are frequent throughout the work. Most of the movements are in some type of closed form, and the contrasting Trio in march style in the third movement is noteworthy.

It is unfortunate that this work is available only with the clarinet part in C, since few clarinetists in the United States own a clarinet in C or would want to transpose an entire work; this will greatly limit the work's performance. The most critical performance problem is ensemble rhythmic precision.

MEULEMANS, ARTHUR (1 884-1966): Belgium
*Trio (6:30). Brussels: Brogneaux (1933)　　　　(Grade V)
    I. Allegro con espiritu
    II. Poco andante
    III. Allegro ritmico

The score bears a dedication to the Professor of Clarinet at the Royal Conservatory of Brussels, Pierre de Leye, and the work, quite predictably, features the clarinet. Short, non-technical cadenzas open and close the middle movement, and a longer, more virtuoso cadenza exploits the instrument's full range (e to b-flat^3) in the last movement. Though basically tonal, Meulemans modulates freely and often to distantly related keys. The cantabile mood of the slow movement offers a contrast to the spirited character of the fast movements.

Except for the cadenzas mentioned above for clarinet, there is an interesting balance in difficulty and musical interest among the parts. The variety of textures demands close attention to precision in entrances, but technical demands are only somewhat difficult.

MEULEMANS, ARTHUR (1884-1966): Belgium (Continued)
*Deuxième trio (15:00). Brussels: CeBeDeM (1960)
(Grade VI)
I. Allegro moderato
II. Adagio
III. Allegro spiritoso

Although much of the melodic and harmonic element of this piece is made up of tertian-based material, tonal centers are rarely delineated. Equal interest is maintained in all of the instruments, but the oboe is particularly prominent in the first movement. The last movement is highly rhythmic and syncopated, and the themes are often based on pentatonic scales.

The foremost problem in the performance of this work would be meeting its technical demands present in all of the parts. An awkward clarinet solo opens the first movement, scored in the instrument's altissimo register. The full range of the reeds is utilized with the clarinet scored up to a-sharp^3. Rhythm presents very few problems, but much of the last movement is written in a concerted fashion requiring precision and uniformity of execution.

MIGOT, GEORGES (1891-   ): France
*Thrène (1:30). Paris: Leduc (1946)   (Grade III-IV)

This unusual little piece, marked "Hiératique et funèbre, " is dedicated to Fernand Oubradous and "To the Memory of Deceased Musicians. " In keeping with the dedication, its mood is somber and mournful, and the harmonies are tense and chromatic.

There are few technical demands made upon the players, except in the oboe where the extremes of its range are emphasized. If the work were much longer it might present serious endurance problems, for there are no rests in any of the parts. The echo effects called for also demand good dynamic range and control. Clarinet in A is required throughout, and three full scores are provided.

*Trio (18:30). Paris: Leduc (1946)   (Grade VI)
I. Prélude
II. Pastorale
III. Chorale
IV. Fanfare et marche
V. Conclusion

A wide variety of textures is used throughout, and many passages are scored for only one or two instruments. Other prominent features of the work are its chromatic harmony, complex rhythm, and modal melodies.

The length of this work will be a factor in its preparation for performance; endurance in the oboe part could be a problem. The melodic writing for the double reeds is particularly angular, while the altissimo register of the oboe is fully utilized up to g^3. The ornaments, particularly mordents, scattered throughout the work are awkward to incorporate smoothly into the melodic lines. Clarinet in A is required throughout.

MIHALOVICI, MARCEL (1898-   ): France
　　Trio, Op. 71 (12:00). Berlin: Ahn and Simrock (c1961)   (Grade VI)
　　　　I. Allegro piacevole
　　　　II. Variazioni
　　Each of the two movements of this extremely complex work is comprised
of several sections. Multimeters, atonality, and rhythmic vitality characterize
the style, with the attainment of an interesting balance among the three instruments. Mihalovici's melodies are remarkably tuneful within his atonal framework.
　　From the standpoint of ensemble precision, this is one of the most
difficult works surveyed in this study; entrances are particularly intricate,
and many passages are scored in octaves or unisons.

MILHAUD, DARIUS (1892-   ): France
　　*Pastorale (4:00). Paris: Le Chant du Monde (1935)   (Grade V)
　　Cast in a ternary form, this short, one-movement work features an
imitative middle section and a highly chromatic, dissonant harmonic style.
Compared with the Suite for reed trio by the same composer, Pastorale
is more abstract and decidedly more dissonant. It is dedicated to the Trio
d'Anches de Paris.
　　Using the composer's suggested metronome markings, the work presents
rather formidable technical challenges. Endurance is of concern to the oboist,
since there are only one and one-half measures rest in the entire piece. All
of the instruments share in the melodic material, and there are no particular
problems regarding range.

　　Suite (d'après Corrette) (8:45). Paris: L'Oiseau-Lyre (1937)
　　　　　　　　　　　　　　　　　　　　　　　　　　　　(Grade IV-V)
　　　　I. Entrée et rondeau
　　　　II. Tambourin
　　　　III. Musette
　　　　IV. Sérénade
　　　　V. Fanfare
　　　　VI. Rondeau
　　　　VII. Menuets (Nos. 1, 2, 3)
　　　　VIII. Le coucou
　　This work is "taken from the incidental music for a production of Romeo
and Juliet, consisting of eight little movements in eighteenth-century style,
based on themes by Michel Corrette. "[15] It is one of the better known works for the
medium and is light in character, tuneful, and only somewhat dissonant.
　　Except for the Menuet No. 1, which features the clarinet, the oboe part
dominates the entire work. The oboist is provided with very few rests in
any of the movements, and the frequent wide, slurred leaps required are
very problematic. A printing error occurs in the first and sixth movements
where the "D. C. " indicated at the end of each movement should read "D. S. "

　　　　　　　　　　*　　　　　*　　　　　*

15. Cobbett, op. cit., p. 38.

53

MOORTEL, ARIE van de (1915-   ): Belgium
    Trio No. 1, Op. 3 (10:00).   Brussels: Maurer (1940)
                                                    (Grade VI)
    I.   Ouverture (Grave; Allegro ben deciso)
    II. Archaique (Allegretto)
    III. Melopee (Molto lento)
    IV. Rondeaux (Presto)
Most of the opening Ouverture is comprised of a fugal treatment of an
angular, multimetric subject (Allegro ben deciso) framed by a slower, and
somewhat more homophonic, Grave.   Short cadenzas in oboe and clarinet
serve as the transition to a modified restatement of the opening Grave
which then closes the movement.   The second movement is basically a
duet for oboe and clarinet employing various modal materials and
frequent harmonic fourths and fifths.   The last movement is very lively
and rhythmical.

     The outer movements are difficult to coordinate in the ensemble due
to the frequent changes of meter, often irregular meters such as 5/8, 7/8,
etc.   Tricky entrances are somewhat simplified by the composer's thoughtful
cross-cueing in the individual parts.   The rhythmical and technical
complexities of the work should challenge the best of players.

MOORTEL, LEO van de (1916-   ): Belgium
    *Divertimento No. 1 (15:00).   Brussels: Maurer (1962)
                                                    (Grade VI)
    I.   Adagio; Allegro moderato
    II. Andantino
    III. Scherzetto (Allegro molto); Trio
    IV. Rondo (Allegro)
Key centers are more clearly delineated in this work than in those of
many other Belgian pieces for the medium.   Melodic chromaticism, however,
is quite frequent throughout.   The second movement employs alternating
phrases and/or sections in 3/4, 5/8, and 4/8.   The more cantabile style of
the Trio of the third movement serves as a contrast to the staccato character
of the rest of the movement.   The Rondo offers a variety of textures and
contrasting sections within its high-spirited mood; a musette-like section
in the middle of the movement is particularly memorable.

     Virtually every serious challenge to a reed trio is present in this work:
technical facility, intricate rhythm, endurance due to the length of the work,
and wide range (particularly for oboe).

    Divertimento No. 3 (15:00).   Brussels: Maurer (1966)
                                                    (Grade V-VI)
    I.   Allegretto
    II. Danse (Allegro moderato)
    III. Blues (Lento moderato; Allegro vivo)
    IV. Finale (Allegro)

The two middle movements are the most unusual and memorable features of this work. The ternary Danse is very witty and rhythmic; the Blues, also in a three-part form, features the clarinet prominently throughout. A jazz influence is evident in much of the piece.

Intricate rhythmic patterns, wide range, and demanding technical facility are the work's main performance problems.

OLSEN, A. LORAN (1930-   ): United States
   *Trio for Woodwinds (7:30). Redondo Beach, California: Composers' Autograph Publications (1957-1958)   (Grade V-VI)
      I. Prelude
      II. Fugato
      III. Song
      IV. Dance

Olsen is presently Associate Professor of Music at Washington State University in Pullman, Washington. He has provided the writer with the following description of this work:

> The piece started out as an experiment in ways to handle tone row material. Each movement of the piece employs a little different juggling of the tone row pitches. The prelude employs three-note harmonic combinations in homophonic style with little more than an awareness of the need for all twelve pitches to be used within a reasonable amount of time. In the fugato the row is handled freely in that, as the notes unfold, other notes may appear in between some of the tone row pitches. The third movement of the song employs a twelve-note row; and then the latter notes of that row (for instance, notes 4-5-7-8-9- and so forth) become the start of a new twelve-note combination, so that the traditional usage of the row in each of the movements is completely changed. Once all twelve notes of the row used for the last movement are exposed they are used in any combination and in any order. Near the end of the last movement there occurs an inverted recapitulation of the opening prelude surrounded by some of the Rondo material inherent in the last movement.[16]

The composer also summarizes the performance problems: "The major obstacle to performing this piece is that of exact ensemble and exact rhythmic placement of the notes. It simply takes a lot of practice for the group to work together and make every eighth note come at the right time."[17]

*   *   *

16. Personal letter written by A. Loran Olsen to the writer on May 2, 1969.
17. Ibid.

ORBAN, MARCEL (1884-1958): France
*Prélude, pastorale, divertissement (9:30). Paris: Editions
du Magasin Musical Pierre Schneider (c1937)   (Grade V)
    I. Prélude (Nostalgique)
    II. Pastorale (Limpide)
    III. Divertissement (Allègre)
This light suite features the cantabile capabilities of the instruments.
All of the first movement is in 5/4 meter, and a dotted rhythmic figure serves
as a unifying device. Chromaticism is frequent, and major-minor modality
is rarely delineated. The work is dedicated to the Trio d'Anches de
Paris.
    Since all three instruments play almost all the time, there are moderate
demands made in endurance. The range in oboe is very wide, and the bassoon
part is quite angular. For the most part, the three instruments are
independent of each other.

PACIORKIEWICZ, TADEUSZ (1916-   ): Poland
*Trio Stroikowe (10:00). Cracow, Poland: Polskie Wydawnictwo
Muzyczne (c1967)   (Grade V)
    I. Allegretto
    II. Lento
    III. Scherzando
    IV. Comodo
    V. Allegro non troppo
Employing a high level of dissonance and an atonal idiom, Paciorkiewicz
achieves contrast from movement to movement by varying the tempo and
texture. The interval of a second, both major and minor, is often used
between two instruments in an accompanying figure. The clarinet alone
begins and ends the second movement, and, in general, thematic material
moves freely from instrument to instrument.
    Ensemble precision is complicated by the independent nature of each of
the instrumental parts and the intricate rhythmic style. The oboe part is
notated on the full score, and this aids the player in coordinating his part
with the others. Melodies range from very narrow, intricate lines to angular,
disjunct contours. Except for some awkward altissimo-register passages for
clarinet near the end of the work, extreme range is rarely employed.

PELEMANS, WILLEM (1901-   ): Belgium
*Trio No. 2 (10:00). Brussels: Maurer (1941) [18]   (Grade IV)
    I. Moderato; Allegro
    II. Andante
    III. Allegro

                    *   *   *
18. Pelemans' Trio No. 1 (1940), published by CeBeDeM, is no longer
published.

Pelemans emphasizes the melodic element with few rhythmic complexities. The harmony is chromatic and somewhat dissonant, and the thematic material is primarily conjunct and moves freely from instrument to instrument.

Except for a brief virtuoso flourish in bassoon near the end, and occasional altissimo-register scoring for oboe and clarinet, the technical demands in this work are only moderately advanced. There are very few ensemble problems, and the multimetric style of the first movement is not problematic, since the same basic duration is maintained throughout.

*Trio No. 3 (7:15). Brussels: Maurer (1960)   (Grade IV-V)
   I. Andantino
  II. Allegretto
 III. Largo
 IV. Allegro

Although this work was written almost twenty years after the second trio, Pelemans' style is much the same. Chromaticism is somewhat more pronounced in this piece, however, and the rhythmic aspect of this work is more varied and lively. The third movement is in 5/4 meter throughout.

A few more technical problems are encountered in this later trio, particularly in the clarinet part. There are few problems in ensemble precision, and the Grade V is based on the clarinet part.

PIERNÉ, PAUL (1874-1952): France
   *Bucolique variée (8:00). Paris: Costallat (c1947)   (Grade V)
As the title suggests, the mood of these free variations is generally light. The work is in five discernable sections with a coda that makes a thematic reference to the opening. The harmonic style is chromatic and only somewhat dissonant. The work is dedicated to the Trio d'Anches de Bruxelles.

Three players of advanced ability are required due to the balance of interest Pierné has written into all of the parts. Unfortunately, the edition is printed poorly; the notes are too small, and there are too many lines per page. This type of printing, coupled with the chromatic style of the music, makes for difficult reading by the players. There are also many discrepancies between the full score and the individual parts with regard to articulation. Although the technical facility demanded of the players is not of virtuoso proportions, that which is called for is quite intricate.

PISK, PAUL A. (1893-   ): Austria
   *Trio, Op. 100 (16:30). New York: Composers Facsimile Edition
   (1960)   (Grade V-VI)
   I. Allegro moderato
  II. Adagio
 III. Allegro
 IV. Vivace

PISK, PAUL A. (1893-   ): Austria (Continued)

Pisk describes his style in this work as "linear, not atonal but free in tonal centers and using the traditional structures and motivic development."[19] The texture used throughout most of the work is contrapuntal. Pisk is now an American citizen and a renowned musicologist. His earlier piece for the same medium, Trio, Op. 18 (1926), is not published.

Because of the contrapuntal nature of most of the work and the use of all three instruments almost constantly, endurance is one of the most critical factors in the work. Multimeters are present in the last movement, and this requires close attention to ensemble rhythmic precision. Technical demands are also advanced.

POOT, MARCEL (1901-   ): Belgium

*Divertimento (6:00). Paris: Eschig (1942)   (Grade IV-V)
    I.   Danza in stilo antico
    II. Canone
    III. Scherzando

The opening movement is somewhat contrapuntal in texture and ternary in form. The contrasting "B" section is not unlike a musette with cantabile melodic material in oboe and clarinet accompanied by a sustained pedal point in bassoon. As the title of the second movement suggests, it is more imitative and serves as a contrast to the highly rhythmic Scherzando which features the oboe prominently. The harmonic idiom is often sharply dissonant.

Although not so difficult as the Ballade discussed below, the performance problems of the present work are concentrated in the last movement where the rhythmic style offers challenges in ensemble precision. Technical demands are only moderate, and there is a balance of interest in all three instruments.

*Ballade (8:30). Paris: Eschig (1954)   (Grade VI)

Poot is one of Belgium's leading contemporary composers and is presently director of the Brussels Conservatory. This piece, which has been characterized as a "vigorous, angular, chromatic showpiece,"[20] is dedicated to the René Daraux Trio d'Anches. It features alternating sections of rhythmic vivacity and disjunct thematic material with slower, more cantabile sections. The harmony is exceedingly chromatic and usually without tonal organization.

The angular, chromatic melodic style presents major problems to the performers. The oboe writing is particularly challenging due to the frequent passages of low-register articulation and awkward, non-idiomatic finger combinations. Many phrases are in octaves, and this type of scoring demands keen attention to accuracy in reading and intonation. The metronome markings in the faster sections seem too fast and would require some alteration for practical performance purposes. There are also printing errors in the rhythmic notation of the clarinet and bassoon parts.

*   *   *

19. Personal letter written by Paul A. Pisk to the writer on June 30, 1969.
20. Rasmussen, Mary, and Mattran, Donald, A Teacher's Guide to the Literature of Woodwind Instruments, p. 192.

QUINET, MARCEL (1915-   ): Belgium
  *Trio à anches (9:00). Brussels: CeBeDeM (1967)
                                                      (Grade V-VI)
      I. Giocoso
     II. Romance
    III. Sicilienne
     IV. Moto perpetuo
    This very substantial piece combines angular melodic material, a
straightforward, but varied, rhythmic style, and an interesting contrast of
textures both within and between movements. The harmonic idiom is
particularly varied with features of tonality within individual lines, bitonality,
and cluster sonorities. The oboe is featured in the second movement with a
difficult, disjunct melody. The constantly recurring sixteenth notes tossed
about from instrument to instrument in the last movement create considerable
momentum.
    A successful performance of the work would require an oboist with expert
control of the altissimo register, agile technique from all three players, and
careful attention to balance and ensemble rhythmic precision in the first and
last movements.

RIISAGER, KNUDAGE (1897-   ): Denmark
  *Conversazione, Op. 26a (8:00). Copenhagen: Engstrom and
    Sodring (1932)   (Grade IV-V)
      I. Allegretto leggiero
     II. Andante moderato
    III. Moderato; Allegro scherzando
    The work opens with bassoon alone in a ten-measure statement of the
principal theme of the movement. It is typical of the composer's melodic
writing with its unexpected rhythmic syncopations and cross rhythms.
An imitative texture predominates throughout most of the outer movements,
and there is a balance of melodic material among the three instruments.
Major and minor scales form the basis for most of the melodies, and
modulations are frequent and abrupt. The plaintive character of the slow
movement is in direct contrast to the lively, animated style of the faster
movements.
    Ensemble rhythmic precision is the most serious problem in this work
due to the syncopated and varied rhythmic style. The chromatic lines require
careful attention, although technical demands are not particularly formidable.
Clarinet in A is required throughout.

RIVIER, JEAN (1896-   ): France
  *Petite suite (9:15). Paris: Fougères (1934)   (Grade V-VI)
      I. Humoresque
     II. Idylle
    III. Valse
     IV. Depart

RIVIER, JEAN (1896-   ): France (Continued)
Rivier combines features of both classicism and impressionism in that formal clarity and chords in parallel motion are evident in the work. The prevailing mood is light and witty, and considerable emphasis is placed on straightforward melodic writing. The work is dedicated to the Trio d'Anches de Paris.
Clarinet in A is needed throughout the first two movements, while B-flat clarinet is used for the remainder of the work. Changing instruments in the middle of the work can have the unfortunate effect of breaking the continuity of the piece as a whole, in addition to creating tuning problems for the clarinetist. Other demands in the work are fast articulation, complex rhythms, and advanced technical facility. The oboist must also cope with awkward arpeggios and low-register staccato.

ROPARTZ, J. GUY (1864-1955): France
*Entrata e scherzetto (6:00). Paris: Salabert (c1948)
(Grade V-VI)
The opening of this work is contrapuntal, chromatic, and sharply dissonant. The following Scherzetto is more rhythmic, but similar to the first movement with regard to texture, harmony, and level of dissonance. Its thematic material is based primarily on a descending, chromatic eighth-note figure stated first in the oboe; several homophonic episodes serve to lighten an otherwise polyphonic texture. The work is dedicated to a contemporary, French composer-conductor, Marcel Labey.
The Scherzetto would be virtually impossible to perform at the suggested metronome markings. Although the instrumental writing is idiomatic, the rhythmic pace and chromatic themes combined offer a formidable challenge to all three players. The lively tempo and contrapuntal texture of the last section present challenges in achieving ensemble precision.

ROSSEAU, NORBERT (1907-   ): Belgium
*Trois jouets, Op. 53 (11:00). Brussels: CeBeDeM (1954)
(Grade V)
    I. Calme avec sérénité
   II. Andante
  III. Allegro
The first movement is written in a Siciliano rhythm and the oboe and clarinet are prominent. The following two movements are less tonal and use a variety of rhythmic ideas and scale materials. The melodies of the final movement are derived from chromatic lines and unusual arpeggio and scale patterns.
Few rests are provided in any of the three parts in the first movement. Range is problematic for oboe in the middle movement where the full range, with several instances of e^3, is exploited. The unusual construction of the thematic material of the last movement requires sound technique and considerable agility.

ROYE, EVARIST de (1907–   ): Belgium
*Trio (11:00). Antwerp: Metropolis (c1956)   (Grade IV-V)
    I. Largo
    II. Andante
    III. Scherzo

The first movement is in rounded binary form, and an imitative texture is used in the contrasting "B" section. Texture is also employed as the principal element of contrast in the Andante's ternary form. Emphasis on rhythm is delayed until the Scherzo; the harmony is tonal and quite straightforward.

The composer's suggested metronome marking in the last movement is challenging, particularly since frequent use is made of the bassoon's altissimo register.

RUEFF, JEANINE (1922–   ): France
*Trois pièces (11:40). Paris: Leduc (c1960)   (Grade VI)
    I. Allegretto scherzando
    II. Andantino espressivo
    III. Allegro (quasi presto)

These pieces are typical of many twentieth-century instrumental works by Paris Conservatory composers. The emphasis is upon technical display, fast-paced rhythmic motion, and a complex, chromatic harmonic idiom. Brackets are used as a notational device to frame important melodic material. This practice is also found in other French works for the medium. The cantabile character of the middle movement affords a needed contrast to the rhythmic and harmonic intensity of the outer movements. The rhythmic aspect of the work is very complex; multimeters, cross rhythms, and a wide variety of rhythmic figures are present.

The style characteristics of the work mentioned above are also the most problematic performance considerations. Ensemble precision in the outer movements is complicated by the intricate rhythmic style. The third movement opens with a passage written in octaves, and thus requires careful attention to intonation and ensemble precision. The angular, chromatic melodies require expert facility by all three players. This work would demand a considerable amount of rehearsal time for performance.

RUELLE, FERNAND (1921–   ): Belgium
*Autour du chateau (8:15). Brussels: Maurer (c1959)
                                                    (Grade IV-V)
    I. Promenade (Allegro)
    II. Un banc à l'ombre (Tempo di barcarolle)
    III. La grand place (Allegro vivo)

Although the title of this work and the subtitles of the movements imply a descriptive, programmatic piece, such is not the case. The music is somewhat abstract, and, at times, humorous. Frequent use is made of chromatic scales, triads, and major-minor scales in the melodic construction; the harmonic idiom is chromatic. The rhythmic style is uncomplicated and quite straightforward.

RUELLE, FERNAND (1921-   ): Belgium (Continued)

The three parts are equally balanced in difficulty and musical interest. Frequent trills and grace notes tend to complicate certain passages, although the facility required is only moderately advanced. Although the prevailing texture is homophonic, the independent character of the parts requires close attention to ensemble balance and precision.

SAUGET, HENRI (1901-   ): France
   Trio (11:15). Paris: L'Oiseau-Lyre (1947)   (Grade V-VI)
     I. Allegro scherzando
     II. Andantino pastorale
     III. Vivo e rustico
     IV. Choral varié

It is interesting that Sauget's teachers, Joseph Canteloube and Charles Koechlin, also wrote works for the reed trio and, in general, in a similar conservative, melodious style. This work is dedicated to the René Daraux Trio and features a rich, chromatic idiom, closed forms, and sprightly rhythms. The third movement is noteworthy for its folk-like dance character. The chorale tune in the last movement remains intact and audible in one instrument or another while a series of harmonic and rhythmic embellishments complement it.

A serious problem for the players of this work is the lack of breathing places and rests, notably in the first two movements. Technical demands are advanced, but the three parts fit together easily in ensemble.

SCARMOLIN, A. LOUIS (1900-   ): United States
   *A Ghostly Tale (4:30). Oskaloosa, Iowa: C. L. Barnhouse (c1963)
                                                       (Grade III)

The composer has supplied the writer with the following succinct summary of the style of this work: "Style -- Misterioso, Descriptive." Its intended use, he says, is "for amateur or professional groups, for concert programs or even for the pleasure of playing together."[21] A minor mode prevails throughout much of the work with a contrasting middle section in major offering some variety. Oboe and clarinet are often scored in thirds with the bassoon relegated to an accompanimental role most of the time.

Scarmolin has written a large number of instrumental works for public school use, and this work would seem to be typical of those for the junior high school level. Technical and ensemble problems are few in number.

SCHIFF, HELMUT (1893-   ): Germany
   *Divertimento (8:00). Vienna: Doblinger (c1966)   (Grade IV-V)
     I. Allegro vivace
     II. Andante grazioso
     III. Vivace assai
     IV. Moderato assai
     V. Allegro, quasi marcia

            *   *   *

21. Personal letter written by A. Louis Scarmolin to the writer on May 10, 1969.

Showing some of the harmonic and melodic influences of Paul Hindemith, Schiff employs a wide variety of rhythmic materials and uses a triplet figure in each of the movements as a unifying device. Generally, the fast movements are more rhythmic and cheerful than the sombre, lyrical slow movements. There is equal interest among the parts, but the clarinet is particularly prominent in most of the movements.

Although the prevailing texture is homophonic, the three instrumental parts are somewhat independent and demand close attention to ensemble precision. Light, rapid staccato articulation is called for, as is frequent low-register playing in the oboe. Except for a few isolated technical passages for oboe and clarinet in the third movement, the requirements in technical facility are only somewhat advanced.

SCHMIT, CAMILLE (1908-): Belgium
    *Trio (10:00). Nancy, France: Société Anonyme d'Editions de Musique
    (1945)   (Grade V)
      I. Allegro ben marcato-bien rhythmé
     II. Moderato
    III. Allegretto bien rhythmé

Schmit employs an atonal idiom, a variety of textures, and a wide range of rhythmic materials. The first movement is contrapuntal throughout, and the lyric second movement is in 5/8 meter. Most of the last movement features duet scoring in oboe and clarinet, accompanied by the bassoon.

The bassoonist is particularly challenged in this work because of the demands in endurance in the first movement and extended altissimo-register playing in the second movement. A reasonably high degree of facility is required in all of the instruments, while the intricate rhythm of the last movement creates serious ensemble problems.

SCHOEMAKER, MAURICE (1890-1964): Belgium
    *Suite Champêtre (12:30). Brussels: CeBeDeM (1940)
                                        (Grade IV-V)
      I. Andante sostenuto
     II. Allegro moderato
    III. Larghetto
    IV. Allegro assai
     V. Adagietto
    VI. Andantino
   VII. Allegro

Except for occasional harsh dissonances, this suite of short movements is somewhat straightforward. Particularly noteworthy are the third and fifth movements; the former features the clarinet in a lengthy, lyric line accompanied by an ostinato accompaniment in oboe and bassoon; the latter is polytonal throughout. The work is skillfully scored and interest is sustained in all of the parts. There is a short cadenza for clarinet in the last movement.

Rapid staccato articulation and sustained high-register playing in oboe in the second movement are the only severe technical problems encountered in the work.

SCHULHOFF, ERWIN (1894-1942): Czechoslovakia
*Divertissement (15:15). Mainz, Germany: Schott (c1928)
(Grade VI)
    I. Ouverture
   II. Burlesca
  III. Romanzero
   IV. Charleston
    V. Tema con variazioni
   VI. Florida
  VII. Rondino-Finale
The elements of style are so varied in this suite that one must discuss each movement separately. For instance, there is a jazz influence in the Charleston, oriental elements in the last movement, and humor in the Romanzero. The harmonic idiom is equally diverse with atonality, polytonality, and tonal organization all being employed from time to time.

The wide range of styles from movement to movement calls for flexibility and versatility by the performers. Although the most technically challenging movements are the first, second, and fourth, the whole work requires expert players because of the complex melodic writing, difficult rhythms, and taxing range requirements.

SEMLER-COLLERY, JULES (1876-   ): France
*Divertissements (11:00). Paris: Les Editions de Paris (c1953)
(Grade V-VI)
    I. Léger et délicat
   II. Calme et Rêveur
  III. Gai et spirituel
The program below is indicated on the full score:

> Three young fellows are walking cheerfully and enjoy the spring weather, far from the student's life.
> There came on three lovely girls who, in spite of their indifference, disturb the merry boys' chatter, making them dreamy and sentimental.
> But philosophy prevails and our three careless youngsters prefer to go on walking, telling jokes and thinking gaily of the hopeful future.

This is one of the few examples of program music for the medium, and the naive little program above is in keeping with the light, unpretentious character of the suite. Each movement is ternary in form and employs a somewhat chromatic harmonic idiom. Most of the rhythmic interest is in the last movement.

Although the work sounds easy, it presents some problems for each player. The bassoonist gets very little rest in the second movement, and its tessitura throughout is high. There are formidable challenges in technical facility and articulation for each player, and the French preference for the oboe's low register is also evident in this work.

64

SEREBRIER, JOSÉ (1938-   ): Uruguay
   *Suite Canina (10:30).   New York: Southern Music Publishing Co.
   (1957)   (Grade V-VI)
      I.   Elegy to My Dead Dog (Lento espressivo)
      II. Dance of the Fleas (Allegro vivo)
      III. Transformation and Toccata (Lento; Allegro)
This unusual work is a curious combination of influences.   Much of the
thematic and rhythmic material suggests a Latin-American influence, while
the first movement and the opening of the third movement are atonal.   The
second movement is very witty.   Serebrier is now an American citizen and
active as a conductor and composer.

   Descending and ascending glissandi are written for the bassoon, both of
which are unusual effects for the instrument.   Several passages are also
written for it in treble clef.   Technical requirements are more demanding
in the clarinet part than in the other instruments; however, the rapid
articulation and awkward altissimo-register trills for oboe and bassoon
are difficult to execute.

SLAVICKY, KLEMANT (1910-   ): Czechoslovakia
   *Trio (14:00).   Prague: Hudebni Matice (1937)   (Grade VI)
      I.   Largo; Con moto
      II. Vivo
      III. Molto tranquillo
      IV. Presto
The composer provides us with the following notes on the work:

> [The work is] based on the contrasting juxta-position of
> the four movements with respect to the technical and
> virtuosic possibilities of the respective instruments.
> The spirit, influenced by Moravian folk melodies, is but
> slightly felt in the first three movements, but in the last
> movement it becomes more authentic and expressive. [22]

   The motoric rhythm, the frequent use of the third as a melodic interval,
and the "night music" quality of the slow movements all suggest Bartók's
influence.

   The attainment of ensemble rhythmic precision is complicated by the
multimeters, and technical requirements are made more difficult by the
chromatic melodic style.   The quality of the printing is below average.

SMIT, ANDRÉ-JEAN (1937-   ): Belgium
   *Trio (11:00).   Brussels: Maurer (1967)   (Grade IV-V)
      I.   Moderato
      II. Larghetto
      III. Allegretto

                        *   *   *
22. Composer's note on the full score of the work.

SMIT, ANDRÉ-JEAN (1937-   ): Belgium (Continued)

The work opens with a lengthy contrapuntal duet between bassoon and clarinet, and much of the rest of the first movement in contrapuntal in texture. Virtually all of the middle movement is polyphonic, opening with an imitative dialogue between clarinet and oboe. Interest is maintained through the use of a variety of melodic and harmonic materials and frequent changes of texture.

The individual character of each of the instrumental parts makes ensemble precision somewhat complex. Except for a few brief altissimo-register passages for oboe in the Larghetto, technical and range demands are not too advanced.

SMITH, LELAND (1925-   ): United States
  *Trio for Woodwinds (14:00). New York: Composers Facsimile
  Edition (1960)   (Grade VI)
      I.   ♩ = c. 96–100
      II. ♩ = c. 50– 54
      III. Bagatelle
      IV. ♩ = 120–126

Smith teaches composition at Stanford University. Each movement is dissonant, multimetric, and extremely complex rhythmically. Contrapuntal textures prevail, but frequent concerted passages emphasize the percussive use of dissonance. The work is dedicated to Madelaine and Darius Milhaud.

Although ensemble rhythmic precision is the most critical problem, the demands in technical facility are of virtuoso proportions in every part.

SOUFFRIAU, ARAENE (1926-   ): Belgium
  *Trio, Op. 49 (10:45). Brussels: Maurer (1957)   (Grade V-VI)
      I.   Allegro
      II. Adagio
      III. Allegro

After successive statements of the opening theme in oboe, bassoon, and clarinet, the first movement continues contrapuntally to its conclusion. The Adagio is also imitative in texture throughout, and only in the last movement does a lighter, more homophonic style prevail. Melodies are quite angular and chromatic, while vertical sonorities are often comprised of seconds, fourths, and other cluster effects. Frequent changes of meter, 4/4 to 3/4, are present in the outer movements.

Technical requirements for the work's fast movements are advanced, as are the demands made in precise ensemble playing due to the continuous contrapuntal scoring in most of the piece. The middle movement is much less problematic than the rest of the work.

SPISAK, MICHAL (1914-   ): Poland
  *Sonatina (10:00). Cracow, Poland: Polskie Wydawnictwo Muzyczne
  (1946)   (Grade VI)
      I.   Allegro
      II. Andante

66

III. Allegro

Spisak employs a wide variety of textures throughout this work. These range from strictly solo lines, to duets, and full ensemble playing. Nearly all of the melodic material is chromatic and wide in range. Each movement is in a closed form; thematic material presented at the beginning of each movement recurs at the end of the movement, usually in a different instrument and with an altered accompaniment. Except for the expressive quality of the middle movement, the mood of the piece is highly spirited. It is dedicated to the René Daraux Trio d'Anches.

All three instruments are featured in the work; the oboe and clarinet are prominent in the first two movements, and the bassoon opens the last movement with a somewhat lengthy solo passage. Several of the most technically difficult passages are written in octaves, and many of the themes are very angular and rhythmically complex.

SPRATT, JACK (1915-   ): United States
   *Three Miniatures for Three Woodwinds (4:30). Stamford,
   Connecticut: Jack Spratt Music Co. (1945)   (Grade III-IV)
      I. Allegro
      II. Andante
      III. Rondo

These short pieces should serve as a good introduction to twentieth-century music for young players with only moderate technical facility. There are occasional harsh dissonances and passages of polymodality, but the prevailing mood is light and the texture is primarily homophonic.

There is a balance of interest and difficulty in all three instruments, and the work affords an opportunity for less experienced players to develop good habits of ensemble playing.

STALLAERT, ALPHONSE (1920-   ): Holland
   *Epitaphes et bagatelles (10:30). Amsterdam: Donemus (1967)
                                                              (Grade V)

      I.   ♩ = 132
      II. ♩ = 66
      III. ♩ = 120
      IV. ♩ = 54
      V.   ♩ = 69

This is one of the most recent pieces published for the reed trio; its style is dissonant and atonal, its thematic material wide ranging and angular, and the prevailing character decidedly abstract. Rhythmic 'ostinati' are used as unifying devices in the first and third movements, while pointillistic and contrapuntal textures are juxtaposed in the last movement.

Technical flourishes are sporadic, but very demanding when they do occur. The low register of the oboe is frequently used, and much of the bassoon part is in its altissimo register. Only the second and third movements are without great problems in ensemble precision; the dynamic aspect of each movement is critical.

67

STEARNS, PETER PINDAR (1931-   ): United States
   *Five Short Pieces (3:00). New York: Composers Facsimile
   Edition (1961)   (Grade V)
      I. Moderato
      II. Poco allegro
      III. Adagio
      IV. Andante
      V. Allegro

   The work is simply in what I call a paraphrase form. That
   is the second and third, fourth and fifth are all based on the
   material, note for note and in the same order of the first
   piece. You might call it a sort of serial procedure that
   encompasses as its "set" an entire body of music, rather than
   an order of twelve notes. I have used this method often.[23]

   The third and fifth pieces are particularly complex rhythmically, and
the style of this work, as a whole, requires mature players. Melodic lines
are disjunct, rhythmic ensemble is intricate, and the dynamic range is wide.
Stearns is presently on a leave-of-absence from a teaching position at Mannes
College of Music in New York. Only a full score of the work is published.

SUTER, ROBERT (1919-   ): Switzerland
   Divertimento (16:00). Zurich: Edition Modern (1955)
                                                        (Grade VI)
      I. Allegro non troppo
      II. Canzone I
      III. Burlesca
      IV. Canzone II
      V. Allegretto s cherzando
   This complex work is characterized by its atonal structure and varied
textures. The oboe is prominent in the first movement, and the clarinet
closes the fourth movement with a cadenza. Thematic material ranges from
short motivic ideas to longer melodies, such as that which introduces Canzone
II. Most movements are in a free, three-part form. The rhythmic pace
throughout is very active, even in the second and fourth movements where
the titles suggest a more lyric style. Texture in the Burlesca is less thick
and more pointillistic than other sections of the piece.
   The performance factors involved with this work are as complex as its
musical style. All three parts demand players of the highest calibre to cope
with the challenges in range, flexibility, ensemble rhythmic precision, and
technical facility.

                  *   *   *

23. Personal letter written by Peter Pindar Stearns to the writer on
July 6, 1969.

SZALOWSKI, ANTONI (1907-   ): Poland
   *Trio (9:00). London: Chester (c1943)   (Grade V)
      I. Allegro
      II. Andante
      III. Gavotte; Musette
      IV. Allegro
   This work is similar in style to Szalowski's other piece for the medium.
However, a simpler, more homophonic texture prevails here as well as a
greater frequency of parallel chord movement. The Musette section of the
movement consists of a flowing clarinet line accompanied by the expected
pedal point in oboe and bassoon.
   The performance problems are also similar to those in the work below.
The last movement is highly syncopated, and, from the standpoint of ensemble
precision, will require careful rehearsal.

   *Divertimento (5:30). London: Chester (c1956)   (Grade V)
      I. Preludio (Allegro)
      II. Arietta (Andante)
      III. Rondino (Allegro)
   Szalowski's study with Nadia Boulanger may account, in part, for the neo-
classical influences in this work. Emphasis is placed on formal clarity, lively
rhythms, and a somewhat dissonant, though tonally organized, harmonic idiom.
Most of the melodic interest is in the clarinet and oboe parts. A variety of
textures is used in the last two movements, and only the first movement is
consistently contrapuntal. The work is dedicated to the René Daraux
Trio d'Anches.
   Although the harmonic aspect of the work is not too complex, the thematic
material is very chromatic and disjunct, requiring flexibility and control from
all three players. There are also demands in rapid articulation, particularly
for the clarinetist in the third movement.

SZÉKELY, ENDRE (1922-   ): Hungary
   *Divertimento (8:00). Budapest: Zenemukiadó Vállalat (1958)
                                                          (Grade IV)
      I. Prelude
      II. Intermezzo No. 1
      III. Intermezzo No. 2
      IV. Finaletto
   Székely provides an interesting contrast from movement to movement with
a modal-based melodic-harmonic style prevailing. The work opens with a
chant-like theme scored in octaves followed by an elaboration of similar
thematic material in a variety of textures. The clarinet is prominent in
the second movement in a light, frothy character. A short oboe recitative
begins the Intermezzo No. 2. A folk-influenced theme in 7/8 meter, stated
successively in each instrument, is the most important element of the
Finaletto.

SZÉKELY, ENDRE (1922-   ): Hungary (Continued)
Except for the rhythmic ensemble in the last movement this work poses few serious problems in performance. There are occasional instances of altissimo-register playing for bassoon. The technical demands are only moderately advanced for all instruments. One of the most immediately appealing works at this grade level, it should work well with high school players.

TANSMAN, ALEXANDER (1897-   ): Poland; France
*Suite (10:30). Paris: Eschig (c1954)   (Grade V)
    I.   Dialogue
    II. Scherzino
    III. Aria
    IV. Finale; Lento
The slow movements are characterized by their contrapuntal textures, expressive melodies, and modal harmonies. Lively rhythms, ostinato accompaniment figures, and angular thematic material are prominent elements of the second and fourth movements. The Lento coda which closes the work is reminiscent, in mood, of the opening Dialogue.

Although no severe technical demands are made upon any of the instruments, the fast movements present formidable problems in ensemble rhythmic precision due to frequent, intricate tutti rhythms. The prominent oboe part in the Finale requires considerable flexibility from the player due to the wide range of the thematic material.

THIRIET, MAURICE (1906-   ): France
*Lais et virelais (13:10). Paris: Meridian (c1956) (Grade V)
    I.   Andantino pastorale
    II. Adagio espressivo
    III. Allegretto amabile
    IV. Andante doloroso
    V.   Allegretto giocoso
According to a brief note on the score in French, these pieces are musical settings of lais and virelais taken from the Manuscrit de Bayeux.[24] This work is similar to Henri Tomasi's Concert Champêtre for the medium discussed below. Characteristic cadences and melodic patterns from the fourteenth and fifteenth centuries are frequent, particularly in the last movement. The principal melody of the first movement is in a Siciliano rhythm, and the thematic material of the second and third movements is more ornamented and tonal. The oboe is prominent in the third movement. The work is dedicated to the René Daraux Trio d'Anches.

Most of the technical problems occur in the last movement; there are several measures of awkward arpeggios for all the instruments and a brief virtuoso passage for bassoon. The range in bassoon is very wide (to d^2) in its solo in the second movement, and, in general, the oboe's low register is emphasized.

*   *   *

24. Composer's note on the full score, p. 1.

70

TOMASI, HENRI (1901-   ): France
   *Concert Champêtre (9:00). Paris: Lemoine (c1938)
                                                    (Grade V-VI)
   I.   Ouverture (Allegro giocoso)
   II. Minuetto
   III. Bourrée (Décidé)
   IV. Nocturne (Andante)
   V.   Tambourin (Vif)
Almost all melodic and harmonic materials in this work are based upon modes. Instruments are often paired in prominent melodic passages or accompaniment figures. The stylized dances and the modal materials combine to give a pronounced pre-baroque quality to the work. Most of the emphasis in the suite is upon the elements of melody and rhythm. The work is dedicated to the Trio d'Anches de Paris.
   Light, rapid articulation, altissimo-register playing by the oboist, lively tempi, and technical facility are all required for the performance of this work. Intonation could be problematic in the frequent passages written in octaves.

VELDEN, RENIER van der (1910-   ): Belgium
   *Divertimento (11:00). Brussels: CeBeDeM (1957)   (Grade VI)
   I.   Allegretto grazioso
   II. Andante espressivo
   III. Allegro quasi moderato e ritmico
The work opens with clarinet alone, and its angular, wide ranging thematic material is typical of the whole piece. The second movement is contrapuntal and begins with oboe alone. Most of the rhythmic interest is present in the last movement which opens with an introduction in 5/4 meter scored in octaves.
   The atonal melodic style offers the most serious performance challenge, rather than ensemble rhythmic precision. The disjunct lines exploit the full range of each instrument, and the requirements in technical agility approach virtuoso proportions.

VELLERE, LUCIE (1896-1966): Belgium
   *Bagatelles (12:30). Brussels: Maurer (1960)   (Grade V)
   I.   Modérément animé
   II. Sans lenteur
   III. Allègrement
   IV. Assez vite
In keeping with the title, the mood is cheerful, good-humored, and highly rhythmical. A variety of textures is employed; some sections are imitative, others chordal. Harmonies are mostly tertian, but key relationships, harmonic progressions, and melodic construction are all free and unstructured.
   Except for occasional awkward technical flourishes, demands in facility are not too great. The unpredictable thematic material makes for difficult reading, but there are no serious problems in keeping the piece together in ensemble.

VEREMANS, MAURICE (1904-1964): Belgium
   *Trio 1 (8:00). Antwerp: Metropolis (1953)   (Grade IV-V)
     I. Scherzando
    II. Lento cantabile
   III. Allegro con spirito

In contrast to most twentieth-century Belgian composers encountered in this study, Veremans writes in a post-romantic idiom. The harmonies are clearly tonal and coloristic; chromatic chords and distantly related modulations are frequent. The melodic writing in the second movement is particularly expressive. The work is dedicated to the Gentse Wind Trio of Belgium.

Players with a good command of major and minor scales and arpeggios will find the technical requirements of this work of a conventional type. The last movement is the most difficult due to its spirited tempo and the independent character of each of the parts. There is a balance of difficulty and musical interest among the parts.

VERESS, SANDOR (1907-): Hungary
   *Sonatina (8:30). Milan: Suvini Zerboni (1931)   (Grade VI)
     I. Allegro giocoso
    II. Andante
   III. Grave; Allegrissimo

> The music reveals a considerable influence of Bartok, not only in a similar shifting modality and rhythmic drive, but also in its general approach to the use of Hungarian folk material. Curiously, parts of the Veress piece in turn anticipate sections of Bartok's Mikrocosmos. [25]

Ensemble rhythmic precision is the most difficult performance problem in this work. Complex multimeters are frequent in the last two movements, and each player's part is rhythmically intricate. Demands in technical facility are only moderately advanced.

VILLA-LOBOS, HEITOR (1887-1959): Brazil
   *Trio (22:00). Paris: Eschig; New York: International (1921)
                                  (Grade VI)
     I. Animé
    II. Languissament
   III. Vivo

> Villa-Lobos has written a trio of staggering complexity and difficulty that is only equalled in his wind quintet; some time is needed to unravel its intricacies, but once penetrated its strange world of bumping 'ostinati', of stammering repetitions broken by swirling scales, and of thickly knotted rhythms holds a strange fascination. [26]

*   *   *

25. Schuller, Gunther, Review in Notes 17:137 Dec 1959.
26. Robertson, Alec, Chamber Music, p. 315.

Of all the works surveyed in this study, this T r i o is one of the most difficult to perform. Its technical demands are of virtuoso proportions, but the most severe challenge is in ensemble rhythmic precision. Clarinet in A is required throughout, and a few passages are written in bass clef. Only the Eschig edition is available with a full score.

VREDENBURG, MAX (1904-   ): Holland
   *T r i o (7:00). Amsterdam: Donemus (1965)   (Grade VI)
      I. Vivo
     II. Affettuoso
    III. Gioviale

The first movement is through-composed, and most of the melodic material is motivic and fragmentary. A lengthy, cantabile oboe solo opens the second movement followed by brief solo passages for the other instruments. The entire work is atonal, multimetric, and very complex rhythmically.

This is one of the most difficult works for the medium. Technical demands are of virtuoso proportions, and ensemble rhythmic precision in the outer movements is difficult to attain.

WALKER, RICHARD (1912-   ): United States
   *A i r a n d D a n c e (2:00). Oskaloosa, Iowa: C. L. Barnhouse (1959)
                        (Grade III-IV)

This pleasant, short piece is an example of a good quality work at the medium level of difficulty. The Air is lyric featuring the clarinet and oboe, and its harmonies are only somewhat chromatic. The Dance is more sprightly and, again, the treble reeds are prominent. The role of the bassoon throughout most of the work is accompanimental. The composer has supplied the writer with the following description of his composition: "Air and Dance is of the romantic idiom; which is my accepted idiom. It is not a highly emotional piece, but rather one which I feel adequately exemplifies the tonal and individualistic properties of this specific small ensemble."[27]

Except for some tied rhythmic figures and staccato articulation in clarinet and oboe, the technical requirements of this work are quite minimal. From the standpoint of the players' interest, it is unfortunate that the bassoonist does not share more in the important melodic material. Range is of concern only in the oboe where its slow-responding low register is occasionally used.

*   *   *

27. Personal letter written by Richard Walker to the writer on May 16, 1969.

WALKER, RICHARD (1912-   ): United States (Continued)
  *Rococo (1:30). Delevan, New York: Kendor (1961)   (Grade III-IV)
  The composer has given the writer the following description of this piece:

> Rococo is in the so-called contemporary idiom. In this
> piece I deliberately avoided harmony on the whole, but
> maintained rhythmic and melodic continuity with an
> emphasis on humor -- all to provide the latter in a presen-
> tation which would be congruent, substantial and thereby
> acceptable. Perhaps I meant the humoristic element to
> be imposed upon the idiom, itself, as if in rebuke.[28]

Walker has written two of the best works for this grade level, and, as he
suggests in his account of the work, this one is more dissonant and rhythmically
active than the earlier Air and Dance. It is technically accessible by
high school players, and it should serve as a good introduction to contemporary
style. The bassoon is prominent, and all three instruments are well balanced
in interest.

WALTHEW, RICHARD H. (1872-1951): England
  *Triolet in E-flat (10:00). London: Boosey and Hawkes (c1934)
                                                        (Grade IV)
    I.   Allegro comodo
    II. Lento, poco appassionato
    III. Intermezzo (Allegretto)
    IV. Vivace

This work is written in a post-romantic style often associated with many
English composers in the twentieth century. Its harmonies are tonal, but
modulations often involve distantly related keys. The second movement
features a poignant oboe melody in rubato style.
  The key to the proper interpretation of this work is careful ensemble
control of rubatos and other nuances in tempo. Demands in range and
technique are only moderately advanced. There is a balance of interest
among the parts, and each instrument is featured prominently from time
to time. Several passages in the second movement are scored in octaves
and require careful attention to intonation.

WATERS, CHARLES (1895-   ): England
  *Serenade (6:30). London: Hinrichsen (c1966)   (Grade IV-V)
    I.   Allegro
    II. Andantino
    III. Larghetto
    IV. Scherzetto
    V.   Vivace

                    *   *   *

28. Ibid.

Employing a homophonic texture throughout, the piece is characterized by lyric, expressive slow movements, chromatic harmonies, and melodic materials frequently based on arpeggiated ninth and eleventh chords.

The oboe is featured in the second movement, and its altissimo register demands sensitive control. There is a balance of interest among the parts, but the oboe is treated a bit more soloistically. The opening measures are scored in octaves, and this demands particular attention to ensemble tuning.

WAXMAN, DONALD (1925-   ): United States
    *T r i o (22:00). New York: Galaxy (1960)   (Grade VI)
        I.   Comodo
        II. Andante
        III. Introduction: Allegro; Allegro vivace

This is one of the longest works for the medium, and its style reveals an interesting blend of influences. The rhythms are lively and syncopated, and many figures can be traced to jazz origins. The harmonies are tertian-based, and ninth and eleventh chords are frequently incorporated into the rich, chromatic idiom. The melodic writing is vigorous and tuneful.

The published score and parts for this work are reproduced from the composer's manuscript, and there are scattered mistakes in rhythmic notation and occasional difficulties in reading the notation. There are serious problems in ensemble precision in every movement, and the complicated rhythmic style and challenging technical demands require players with advanced facility. The extended performance time involved is also an important consideration in performing it.

WEBER, ALAIN (1930-   ): France
    *T r i o d' a n c h e s (8:30). Paris: Leduc (c1956)   (Grade V-VI)
        I.   Allegro moderato
        II. Lent et expressif
        III. Vif et léger (Fugue)

The clarinet alone opens the work with a rhythmic statement of an atonal theme which is answered imitatively in oboe and bassoon. A more lyric theme in oboe later affords thematic contrast, and the rest of the movement juxtaposes these two themes and develops motives derived from them. The second movement is scored as one large crescendo and decrescendo with the dynamic and melodic climax coming near the middle of the movement; a quasi-ostinato pattern in eighth-notes serves as a unifying feature. The contrapuntal texture of the last movement is implied by its subtitle. The nine-measure fugue subject, stated first in the bassoon, hints at the key of f-sharp minor, but the listener must wait until the end of the movement before the key is clearly defined.

The contrapuntal textures, angular, chromatic thematic material, and endurance in the double reeds are the most critical performance factors in this work. There is a short cadenza for clarinet near the middle of the last movement, and a sustained g-sharp^3 for the same instrument occurs at the end.

WERNER, JEAN-JACQUES (1935-   ): France
    Trio d'anches (13:45). Paris: M. R. Braun (c1962) (Grade V)
        I.   Allegro moderato
        II. Andante
        III. Scherzo
        IV. Final-Allegro
Werner features the bassoon prominently in each of the four movements.
The chromatic idiom borders on atonality at times. The texture is mostly
homophonic, while the rhythmic style occasionally shows possible jazz
influence in the outer movements. Rhythmic patterns also serve to unify
certain movements; a recurring dotted figure in the first movement and a
motoric clarinet ostinato in the Final-Allegro are good examples of such
patterns.

Flexibility in tempo, endurance, and technical facility are the principal
performance problems encountered in this work. Several different tempo
indications are present in succession in the first movement, and a wide
variety of rhythmic figures is found throughout. The tempo indicated by
the metronome marking of the Scherzo is extremely challenging, and the
frequent use of accidentals complicates reading.

WILDBERGER, JACQUES (1922-   ): Switzerland
    *Trio (13:00). Munich: Edition Modern (1953)   (Grade VI)
        I.   Introduzione; Monodia; Polifonica
        II. Hoquetus; Recitativa; Conclusione
Many of Wildberger's works are organized according to principles of
serialism with underlying mathematical interrelationships of notes, intervals,
and rhythm. A detailed analysis of this work would probably reveal a similar
organization in sections of this work. Themes range from short, disjunct
motives to longer, more conjunct lines with fleeting references to tonal
organization; however, the prevailing harmonic idiom is decidedly atonal.
The titles of the sections serve to suggest their texture and character. For
instance, the Polifonica is considerably more contrapuntal than other sections
of the work, while the theme in the Hoquetus is fragmented among the three
instruments much as in the practice called hocket in thirteenth- and fourteenth-
century polyphonic music.

A limiting factor in the performance of this work is that no individual parts
are published; only a full score with the clarinet part in C is available.
Coupled with its formidable challenges in ensemble precision, range, rhythmic
complexity, and technical facility, this piece must be regarded as one of
the most difficult for the medium.

WISSMER, PIERRE (1915-   ): Switzerland
    *Sérénade (7:00). Paris: Costallat (1938)   (Grade IV)
        I.   Prélude
        II. Chanson
        III. Danse

Wissmer is usually regarded as a neo-classical composer. This work combines a homophonic texture, multimeters, melodies derived from modal and tonal materials, and occasional pre-baroque effects, such as Landini cadences.

Except for the wide range in oboe and the changing meters in the Danse, there are no severe performance problems in this work. A high school trio should find it a worthwhile challenge, and an ensemble of any level would benefit from its study and performance. Clarinet in A is required throughout.

WOESTYNE, DAVID van de (1915-   ): Belgium
   *Divertimento (13:00). Brussels: CeBeDeM (1941)   (Grade IV-V)
      I. Inleiding en fugato
      II. Intermezzo
      III. Molto lento
      IV. Allegro molto

Woestyne combines a variety of textures, a somewhat chromatic (although always tonal) harmonic style, and a wide range of moods in this straightforward and uncomplicated work. The first and third movements are somewhat contrapuntal, chromatic, and even share similar thematic material. The other movements feature the oboe prominently and are noteworthy for their light, rhythmic character. The composer favors duet scoring in oboe and clarinet, usually in parallel thirds, and the bassoon is often relegated to an accompanimental role.

The contrapuntal texture of the slow movements requires close attention to balance, and a wide dynamic range is present in each movement. Rapid, staccato articulation and a reasonably advanced technique are demanded in the faster movements. There are very few rhythmic ensemble problems.

ZANABONI, GIUSEPPE (1926-   ): Italy
   *Piccola Suite (10:40). Padova, Italy: Zanaboni (c1967)
                                                    (Grade IV-V)
      I. Preludio (Larghetto)
      II. Scherzo (Allegro)
      III. Canzone triste (Adagio espressivo)
      IV. Finale alla marcia (Con spirito parodistico)

This work is the only one for the medium by an Italian-born composer included in this survey. The vertical texture is generally dissonant and atonal. The first and third movements are very expressive and void of any tonal organization or tertian-based chordal and melodic construction. On the other hand, the faster movements, although by no means tonal, do make use of the melodic and harmonic third and fifth.

Only a full score, with the clarinet part in C, is published for this piece, and this could present a serious problem to players wanting to program it. Not only would two other scores have to be purchased or duplicated, but the problem of transposition of the clarinet part is a critical one. Several passages for bassoon are scored either in tenor or treble clef, while technical demands are moderately advanced.

ZBINDEN, JULIEN-FRANÇOIS (1917-   ): Switzerland
   *Trio, Op. 12 (14:00). Paris: Lemoine (1949)   (Grade V-VI)
      I. Ricercare
      II. Divertimento
      III. Tema con variazioni

      Each one of the instruments follows its own line, completely
      free as to tempo. The first movement is a very slow
      Ricercare, which has nothing of the fugue-inspired form
      that this title carries with it.   Three melodic lines are
      superimposed.   The Divertimento that follows has a
      certain 'bonhomie' about it, and is full of animation,
      which is hardly interrupted at all by the introduction of a
      few bars of an Andante sostenuto.   The Finale presents
      six short variations on a pastoral theme of eleven bars,
      the last variation being a progressive resolution of the
      theme.   The whole corresponds very well with what is
      expected from a trio of reed instruments: pleasing music,
      without any pretention to lyrical or dramatic effects. [29]

The work is dedicated to the André Dupont Trio d'Anches.
      The rhapsodic nature of the first movement requires careful ensemble
coordination. Ensemble rhythmic precision is a challenge in every movement
due to the multimeters and the constantly changing basic duration.   The
altissimo register of the bassoon is fully utilized.

                     *   *   *

29. Swiss Composers' League, 40 Contemporary Swiss
Composers, pp. 214-15.

                              78

BIBLIOGRAPHY

ALTMANN, Wilhelm. Kammermusik-Katalog. Leipzig: F. Hofmeister, 1945. 400p

AMERICAN Society of Composers, Authors and Publishers. The ASCAP Biographical Dictionary of Composers, Authors and Publishers. New York: The Society, 1966. 845p

BAINES, Anthony. Woodwind Instruments and Their History. New York: W. W. Norton Co., 1963. 382p

BAKER'S Biographical Dictionary of Musicians, 5th ed. Completely revised by Nicolas Slonimsky. New York: G. Schirmer, 1958. 1855p

BRITISH Broadcasting Corporation Music Library. Chamber Music Catalogue. London: The Corporation, 1965.

BULL, Storm. Index to Biographies of Contemporary Composers. New York: Scarecrow Press, 1964. 405p

CAMDEN, Archie. Bassoon Technique. London: Oxford University Press, 1962. 74p

COBBETT, Walter Willson, ed. Cyclopedic Survey of Chamber Music, 2nd ed., vol. 3. London: Oxford University Press, 1963.

DAVIES, J. H. Musicalia. London: Pergamon Press, 1966. 218p

DUNHILL, Thomas F. Chamber Music. London: Macmillan Co., 1925. 311p

EWEN, David. European Composers Today. New York: H. H. Wilson, 1954. 200p

FÉTIS, Francois J. Biographie universelle des musiciens et bibliographie générale de la musique, 2nd ed., vol. 5. Paris: Firmin Didot Freres, 1863.

GORGERAT, Gérald. Encyclopédie pour instruments à vent, 2nd ed., vol. 3. Lausanne: Editions Rencontre, 1955.

HELLER, George N. Ensemble Music for Wind and Percussion Instruments: A Catalog. Washington: Music Educators National Conference, 1970. 142p

HELM, Sanford Marion. Catalog of Chamber Music for Wind Instruments. Ann Arbor, Michigan: Braun-Brumfield, 1952. 85p

HOUSER, Roy. Catalogue of Chamber Music for Woodwind Instruments. Bloomington, Indiana: Indiana University, 1962. 159p

KROLL, Oskar. The Clarinet. Translated by Hilda Morris. New York: Taplinger Publishing Co., 1968. 183p

LARSEN, Knud, ed. The Society for Publishing Danish Music (SAMFUNDET) Catalogue. Copenhagen: The Society, 1956. 64p

LATIN-AMERICAN Music Available at Indiana University. Bloomington, Indiana: Indiana University, School of Music, 1964. 101p

MICHEL, François, ed. Encyclopédie de la musique. 3 vols. Paris: Fasquelle, 1958-1961.

MUSIC Educators National Conference. Materials for Miscellaneous Instrumental Ensembles. Washington, D. C.: The Conference, 1960. 89p

NATIONAL Interscholastic Music Activities Commission. Selective Music Lists. Washington, D. C.: The Commission, 1965. 178p

OPPERMAN, Kalmen. Repertory of the Clarinet. New York: Ricordi, 1960. 140p

PERSICHETTI, Vincent. Review of Mabel Daniels, Three Observations for Three Woodwinds. Notes 11:157 Dec 1953.

RASMUSSEN, Mary, and MATTRAN, Donald. A Teacher's Guide to the Literature of Woodwind Instruments. Durham, New Hampshire: Brass and Woodwind Quarterly, 1966. 226p

REIS, Claire R. Composers in America. New York: Macmillan Co., 1947. 399p

RENDALL, F. Geoffrey. The Clarinet. London: Ernest Benn, 1954. 184p

RICHTER, Johannes Friedrich. Kammermusik-Katalog. Leipzig: F. Hofmeister, 1960. 318p

ROBERTSON, Alec. Chamber Music. Baltimore: Penguin, 1960. 427p

ROSENTHAL, Lawrence. Review of Jean Francaix, Divertissement. Notes 12:641 Sept 1955.

ROTHWELL, Evelyn. Oboe Technique. London: Oxford University Press, 1953. 106p

SCHUH, Willi and others. Schweizer Muker-Lexicon, Dictionnaire des musicienes suisses. Zurich: Atlantis Verlag, 1964. 421p

SCHULLER, Gunther. Review of Sándor Veress, Sonatina. Notes 17:137 Dec 1959.

SWISS Composers' League. 40 Contemporary Swiss Composers. Bodensee: Verlag Amriswil, 1956. 222p

VOXMAN, Himie; ANDERSON, Paul; and DAVIS, Thomas. Selected Wind and Percussion Materials. Iowa City: University of Iowa, School of Music, 1965. 130p

WESTPHAL, Frederick W. Guide to Teaching Woodwinds. Dubuque, Iowa: W. C. Brown Co., 1962. 315p

PUBLISHERS

Agents in the United States for foreign publishers are indicated in parentheses.

Ahn & Simrock, Schützenhofstrasse 4, Wiesbaden 62, Germany
Amphion, Edition Musicales, 5 Rue Jean Ferrandi, Paris 6, France (Belwin-Mills)
Associated Music Publishers, 609 Fifth Avenue, New York, N. Y. 10017
Barnhouse, C. L., 110 B. Avenue, Oskaloosa, Iowa 52577
Baron, Maurice, Box 149, Oyster Bay, N. Y. 11771
Belwin-Mills, Inc., Rockeville Centre, Long Island, N. Y. 11571
Boosey & Hawkes, 209 Victor Street, Oceanside, N. Y. 11572
Braun, M. R., Paris, France (M. Baron)
Brogneaux, 73 Paul Janson Laan, Brussels, Belgium (Henri Elkan)
CeBeDeM, Rue de Commerce 3, Brussels, Belgium (Henri Elkan)
Chant du Monde, Le, 32 Rue Beaujon, Paris, France (Leeds)
Chester, J. & W., 11 Great Marlborough Street, London W. 1, England
Columbo, Franco, c/o Belwin-Mills, Inc., Rockeville Centre, Long Island, N. Y. 11571
Composers' Autograph Publications, 1527 1/2 N. Vine Street, Hollywood, Calif. 90068
Composers Facsimile Edition, 170 West 74th Street, New York, N. Y. 10023
Concordia Publishing House, 3558 South Jefferson Avenue, St. Louis, Mo. 63118
Costallat, 60 Rue de la Chausee-d'Antin, Paris, France (M. Baron)
Dania Edition, Copenhagen, Denmark (C. F. Peters)
Doblinger, Ludwig, Dorotheergasse 10, Vienna, Austria (Associated)
Donemus, Jacob Obrechtstraat 51, Amsterdam, Holland (C. F. Peters)
Durand Edition, 4 Place de la Madelaine, Paris, France (Presser)
Elkan, Henri, 1316 Walnut Street, Philadelphia, Pa. 19107
Elkan-Vogel, Theodore Presser, Presser Place, Bryn Mawr, Pa. 19010
Engstrom & Sodring, Copenhagen, Denmark (C. F. Peters)
Eschig, Max, 48 Rue de Rome, Paris, France (Associated)
Fischer, Carl, 62 Cooper Square, New York, N. Y. 10003
Fourgères, Paris, France
Galaxy Music Corp., 2121 Broadway. New York, N. Y. 10023
Gallet, 6 Rue Vivienne, Paris, France (H. Elkan)
General Music Publishing Co., 414 East 75th Street, New York, N. Y. 10021
Hinrichsen Edition, 25 Museum Street, London WC. 1, England (C. F. Peters)
Hudebni Matice, Prague, Czechoslovakia (Boosey & Hawkes)
Kendor Music, Inc., Delevan, N. Y. 14042
Kistner & Siegel, Dorrienstrasse 13, Leipzig C. 1, Germany (Concordia)
Krenn, Wien, Germany
Leduc, Alphonse, 175 Rue St. Honore, Paris 1, France (M. Baron)
Leeds, 445 Park Avenue, New York, N. Y. 10022

Lemoine, Henri, 17 Rue Pigalle, Paris, France (Presser)
Lienau, Robert, Lankwitzerkstrasse 9, Berlin, Germany (C. F. Peters)
L'Oiseau-Lyre, 122 Rue de Grenelle, Paris 9, France
Marks, E. B., G. Schirmer, 609 Fifth Avenue, New York, N. Y. 10017
Maurer, Editions J., Avenue du Verseau 7, Brussels 15, Belgium
MCA Music Corp., 445 Park Avenue, New York, N. Y. 10022
Meridian, Les Nouvelles Editions, Paris, France
Metropolis, Editions, Van Ertbornstraat 5, Antwerp 1, Belgium (Henri Elkan)
Modern, Edition, Zurich, Switzerland, also Munich, Germany (General Mus.
   Pub.)
Noetzel, O. H., Wilhelmshaven, Germany (C. F. Peters)
Paris, Les Editions de, Paris, France
Peters, C. F., 373 Park Avenue, New York, N. Y. 10016
Presser, Theodore, Presser Place, Bryn Mawr, Pa. 19010
Polskie Wydawnictwo Muzyczne, Cracow, Poland (E. B. Marks)
Richard, Paul, Paris, France
Ricordi, Edition, Worldwide locations (Belwin-Mills)
Rubank, 5544 West Armstrong Avenue, Chicago, Ill. 60646
Salabert, 22 Rue Chauchat, Paris 9, France (Belwin-Mills)
Schirmer, G., 609 Fifth Avenue, New York, N. Y. 10017
Schneider, Editions du Magasin Musical Pierre, 61 Avenue Raymond-Poincare,
   Paris 16, France
Schott, B. Sohne, Weihergarten 5, Mainz, Germany (Belwin-Mills)
Selmer, Edition, 4 Place Dancourt, Paris, France (M. Baron)
Sikorski, Hans, Hamburg, Germany (Belwin-Mills)
Simrock, N., Taubchenweg 20, Leipzig, Germany (Associated)
Skandinvisk og Borups, 31 Bredg., Copenhagen, Denmark
Societé Anonyme d'Editions, 7 Rue Gombetta, Nancy, France
Southern Music Co., 1100 Broadway, San Antonio, Texas 78206
Southern Music Publishing Co., 1619 Broadway, New York, N. Y. 10019
Suvini Zerboni, 4 Galleria del Corso, Milan, Italy (MCA)
Spratt, Jack, Box 277, Old Greenwich, Conn. 06870
Transatlantiques, Editions Musicales, 14 Avenue Hoche, Paris 8, France
   (Theodore Presser)
Zanaboni, G. C., 24 p. Unita d'Italia, Padua, Italy (C. F. Peters)
Zenemúkiadó Vállalat, Budapest, Hungary (Boosey & Hawkes)